W9-DDG-134

TREASURY OF CHINESE COOKING

PUBLICATIONS INTERNATIONAL, LTD.

Copyright © 1994 by Publications International, Ltd.
All rights reserved. This publication may not be reproduced or quoted in whole or in part by mimeograph or any other printed or electronic means, or for presentation on radio, television, videotape or film without written permission from:

Louis Weber, C.E.O.
Publications International, Ltd.
7373 N. Cicero Ave.
Lincolnwood, IL 60646

Permission is never granted for commercial purposes.

Kikkoman is a registered trademark owned by Kikkoman Corporation. All Kikkoman recipes developed and tested by the home economists of the Kikkoman Kitchens.

Front cover photography by Photo/Kevin Smith, Chicago.

Pictured on the front cover: Chicken Chow Mein *(page 120)*.

ISBN: 0-7853-0798-2

Library of Congress Catalog Card Number: 94-66823

Manufactured in U.S.A.

8 7 6 5 4 3 2 1

Microwave Cooking: Microwave ovens vary in wattage. The microwave cooking times given in this publication are approximate. Use the cooking times as guidelines and check for doneness before adding more time. Consult manufacturer's instructions for suitable microwave-safe cooking dishes.

CONTENTS

INTRODUCTION

Chinese Cooking, as we know it, is actually a combination of cooking techniques and seasonings from all the regions of China. Northern or Beijing cooking features wheat noodles, dumplings, sweet-sour sauces, garlic and green onions. The coastal areas around Shanghai are known for their fabulous seafood and delectable sauces. Szechuan and Hunan cooking use a blend of seasonings to create dishes that have a combination hot, sour, sweet, salty taste all in one bite. Southern or Cantonese cooking, which is mildly seasoned and frequently served in Chinese-American restaurants, emphasizes cooking with soy sauce, ginger and sherry. We have taken the best from these regions to include in this publication.

Cooking Techniques

Although a variety of familiar cooking techniques are used in preparing Chinese dishes, stir-frying, the most popular technique, is featured throughout this book. Before you begin, take a few minutes to read the following information. Stir-frying is easily mastered, and these helpful guidelines will enhance your enjoyment of these wonderful dishes.

Stir-frying involves the rapid cooking of ingredients in a small amount of cooking oil over medium-high heat for a few minutes. In addition to saving time, the quick cooking preserves the nutrients, flavors, textures and colors of the food. Stir-frying can be divided into two separate steps—preparing the ingredients and cooking the ingredients.

It is essential to have all the ingredients prepared in advance. This means all cleaning, cutting, measuring and combining. Stir-frying proceeds so quickly that there is no time to do anything else once cooking begins. When cutting meats and vegetables, make the pieces a uniform shape and size to ensure even cooking.

When you're ready to begin, place a wok or large skillet over medium-high or high heat. Preheating the pan prevents the food from sticking. When a drop of water added to the pan sizzles, the pan is sufficiently hot. Next add the oil, swirling to coat the inside of the pan; heat until the oil is hot, about 30 seconds. Now the ingredients can be added.

Stir-fry the meat first and remove. Then add the vegetables, beginning with those that take the longest to cook. Briskly toss and stir with a flat metal or wooden spatula. Be sure to keep the food in constant motion. This ensures that all surfaces are quickly coated with hot oil to seal in the flavorings, and also prevents overcooking or burning. To maintain the characteristic Chinese tender-crisp quality, serve stir-fried dishes immediately.

The best oils to use for stir-frying are vegetable oils that can withstand intense heat without smoking. Peanut oil, corn oil and soybean oil are excellent choices. Other kinds of fat, such as olive oil, sesame seed oil, butter or lard cannot be used because they have low burning points.

Utensils

A reasonably equipped kitchen usually contains more than enough utensils to adequately handle Chinese cooking. However, one item you may not have, but may wish to consider purchasing, is a wok, especially if you plan to make stir-fried dishes often. Invented centuries ago, the wok is an all-purpose cooking pan used in virtually every Chinese household for almost every kind of cooking.

Traditionally, a wok was made from thin, tempered iron, and had a rounded bottom for fast, even conduction of heat. However, modern technology has brought some changes to the wok. In addition to iron, woks are now manufactured in aluminum, stainless steel and carbon steel. Woks with flat surfaces are made for use on electric ranges and on smooth-top cooking surfaces. There are electric woks with nonstick finishes and automatic thermostatic controls. On some woks, the customary thin metal handles positioned on two sides have been replaced with a long wooden handle. This version eliminates the necessity of keeping pot holders handy at all times to pick up or steady the wok.

Woks range in size from 12 to 24 inches in diameter. The fourteen-inch size is a good choice because it can handle most cooking chores without interfering with the use of other burners on the rangetop.

Before a new iron or carbon steel wok is used, it should be washed and seasoned. Wash it thoroughly in hot, soapy water (the first time only) and use a scouring pad, if necessary, to remove any protective coating. Rinse the wok with water and dry it completely. Rub 1 tablespoon of vegetable oil completely over the interior of the wok. Place it over low heat until hot throughout, 3 to 5 minutes; remove the wok from heat and let cool.

After each use, the wok should be soaked briefly in hot water and cleaned with a bamboo brush or sponge. Do not clean the wok with soap or soap-treated scouring pads. Rinse the wok with water, dry it and place it over low heat until all water evaporates. Then rub 1 teaspoon of vegetable oil over the inside of the wok to prevent it from rusting.

Another very useful utensil for Chinese cooking is a cleaver. While not essential, it is handy for slicing, chopping and mincing ingredients, and is especially helpful for chopping whole chickens and ducks into Chinese-style serving pieces.

Helpful Hints

● When removing stir-fried meat, poultry or seafood from the wok, always place the meat in a clean dish, not the one that held the raw or marinated food.

● Any foods that need to be marinated over 20 minutes should be marinated in the refrigerator.

● Resealable plastic food storage bags are great to use for marinating foods.

● Always have all the ingredients prepared—sliced, measured, marinated, combined—before you begin stir-frying, and have them located close to the wok.

● Stir any cornstarch mixtures before adding them to the hot wok. The cornstarch needs to be dissolved in the liquid to prevent it from lumping.

● Partially freeze beef, pork or poultry to make it easier to slice into thin strips.

● For a no-fuss stir-fry, use vegetables, such as sliced mushrooms, broccoli or cauliflower florets, spinach or bean sprouts from the deli bar of the supermarket *or* frozen mixed vegetables, such as a broccoli and cauliflower combination.

● Use fresh flour tortillas from the supermarket dairy case in place of mandarin pancakes.

● Freeze leftover broth in clean ice cube trays. Once the broth is frozen, remove the cubes and store them in a resealable freezer food storage bag to prevent evaporation. Remove cubes as needed; they can be quickly defrosted in a microwave oven.

● Use prepackaged shredded coleslaw mix or cabbage for egg roll fillings or any other recipes that call for shredded cabbage.

● Use chicken tenders for recipes that call for strips of chicken. Turkey tenders, cutlets and tenderloin can be substituted for chicken cubes or strips.

● Use roasted chicken from the deli department of your local supermarket or vacuum-packed precooked chicken breasts when a recipe calls for cooked chicken.

Ingredients

When preparing Chinese foods, you will come across many ingredients that are familiar. You will also encounter some that may be unfamiliar, such as wood ears, oyster sauce or Chinese five-spice powder. Some of the items—seasonings in particular—may be available only in Chinese food markets. Before you search for an out-of-the-way specialty store, however, check your local supermarket. Many supermarkets now stock good inventories of Chinese ingredients. In addition to canned, bottled or packaged goods, many carry fresh items such as wrappers, bean curd and Chinese-style thin egg noodles. A check of the frozen-food cases will yield additional Chinese items.

As with any other kind of cooking, choose the freshest ingredients you can find, especially when purchasing meat, poultry or fish. The Chinese are so concientious about cooking with the freshest possible foods that they plan their menus around the foods they find in the market—rather than planning the marketing around the menu. The glossary that follows describes many of the Chinese foods used in the recipes in this book.

Bamboo shoots: tender, ivory-colored shoots of tropical bamboo plants, used separately as a vegetable and to add crispness and a slight sweetness to dishes. They are available fresh or in cans and should be rinsed with water before using. Store opened, canned bamboo shoots submerged in water in a covered container in the refrigerator. Every 2 to 3 days, drain and discard the water and replace it with fresh cold water. Bamboo shoots may be kept up to 2 weeks.

Bean sprouts: small white shoots of the pealike mung bean plant, used separately as a vegetable and included in a wide variety of dishes. They are available fresh or in cans. Canned bean sprouts should be rinsed before use to eliminate any metallic taste. Store opened, canned bean sprouts in the refrigerator for up to 5 days. Store fresh bean sprouts in a plastic bag in the refrigerator for about 1 week.

Bean threads (also called cellophane noodles or Chinese rice vermicelli): dry, hard, white fine noodles made from powdered mung beans. They have little flavor of their own but readily absorb the flavors of other foods.

Black beans, fermented: strongly flavored, preserved small black soybeans. They are quite salty and are often used as a seasoning in combination with garlic. Fermented black beans are available in cans, bottles or plastic bags; they should be rinsed or soaked in water before using.

Bok choy: a member of the cabbage family, has white stalks and green, crinkled leaves. The woody stems take longer to cook than the delicate leaf tips. Store in a plastic bag in the refrigerator for up to 4 days.

Chili oil, hot: vegetable or sesame oil that has had hot red chilies steeped in it. This red-colored oil adds heat and flavor to Chinese dishes.

Chili sauce, Chinese: a bright red, extremely spicy sauce made from crushed fresh red chili peppers and salt. It is available in cans or bottles and should be used sparingly.

Egg noodles, Chinese: a thin pasta usually made of flour, egg, water and salt. The noodles can be purchased fresh, frozen or dried.

Egg roll wrappers: commercially prepared dough made of flour and water, rolled very thin and cut into 7- or 8-inch squares. They are available fresh or frozen.

Five-spice powder, Chinese: cocoa-colored powder that is a ready-mixed blend of five ground spices, usually anise seed, fennel seed, cloves, cinnamon and ginger or pepper. It has a slightly sweet, pungent flavor and should be used sparingly.

Ginger (also called gingerroot): a knobby, gnarled root with a brown skin and whitish or light green interior. It has a fresh, pungent flavor and is used as a basic seasoning in many Chinese recipes. Ginger is available fresh and needs to be peeled before using. Store it wrapped in plastic in the refrigerator for about 2 weeks or in a resealable freezer food storage bag for up to 4 weeks. (You may cut off what you need and return the remainder to the freezer.) Or, store peeled ginger covered with dry sherry in an airtight container in the refrigerator for up to 6 months. The sherry absorbs some of the ginger flavor and may be used for cooking.

Hoisin sauce: a thick, dark brown sauce made of soybeans, flour, sugar, spices, garlic, chilies and salt. It has a sweet, spicy flavor and is called for in numerous Chinese recipes. It is available as a prepared sauce.

Lily buds (also called tiger-lily buds or golden needles): long yellow strips which are the flower buds of the tiger lily. They come dried and must be soaked in warm water before using. Lily buds have a slightly musky flavor and are used in soups, stews and vegetarian dishes. They are available in cellophane packages but can be difficult to find; if you can't get them simply omit them from the recipe.

Lychee (also called lichee or litchi): a small, juicy, oval-shaped fruit with a brownish or bright red skin, white pulp and large pit. They are used in main dishes in combination with other foods or served separately as a dessert or snack. Lychees are available in cans—whole, pitted and packed in syrup.

Mushrooms, dried: dehydrated black or brown mushrooms from the Orient, with caps from 1 to 3 inches in diameter. They have a strong distinctive flavor and are included in many different kinds of recipes. Chinese dried mushrooms must be soaked in warm water before using and are usually called for thinly sliced. Store in an airtight container in a cool, dark place. Dried mushrooms are available in cellophane packages.

Napa cabbage: a member of the cabbage family, has elongated tightly furled leaves with wide ribs and soft pale green tips. Store in a closed plastic bag in the refrigerator for up to 5 days.

Oyster sauce: a thick, brown, concentrated sauce made of ground oysters, soy sauce and brine. It imparts very little fish flavor and is used as a seasoning to intensify other flavors. It is available as a prepared sauce.

Parsley, Chinese (also called cilantro or fresh coriander): a strongly flavored green herb with flat broad leaves similar in appearance to Italian or flat-leaf parsley, commonly used fresh as a seasoning or garnish.

Peanut oil: a golden-colored oil pressed from peanuts that has a light and slightly nutty flavor. This oil has a high smoke point that makes it ideal for using in stir-fried recipes. Store it tightly covered in a cool, dark place for up to 6 months after opening.

Plum sauce: a thick, piquant, chutneylike sauce frequently served with duck or pork dishes. It is available as a prepared sauce or can be homemade.

Satay (Saté) sauce (also called Chinese barbecue sauce): a dark brown, hot, spicy sauce composed of soy sauce, ground shrimp, chili peppers, sugar, garlic, oil and sauces. It is available in cans or jars.

Sesame oil: an amber-colored oil pressed from toasted sesame seeds. It has a strong, nutlike flavor and is best used sparingly. Sesame oil is generally used as a flavoring not as a cooking oil because of its low smoke point. Store it tightly covered in a cool, dark place for up to 2 months after opening.

Snow peas (also called pea pods or Chinese peas): flat, green pods that are picked before the peas have matured. They add crispness, color and flavor to foods, require very little cooking and are frequently used in stir-fried dishes. Snow peas are available fresh or frozen. Store fresh snow peas in a plastic bag in the refrigerator for 3 to 4 days.

Soy sauce: a pungent, brown, salty liquid made of fermented soybeans, wheat, yeast, salt and sometimes sugar. It is an essential ingredient in Chinese cooking. There are several types of soy sauce (light, dark, heavy), as well as Japanese-style soy sauce. The Japanese-style sauce is somewhere between the light and dark varieties. All types of soy sauce are available in bottles.

Stir-fry sauce: a prepared sauce that can be added as an instant seasoning to stir-fried dishes.

Sweet and sour sauce: a combination of sugar, vinegar and other flavorings. It is available as a prepared sauce or can be homemade.

Szechuan peppercorns: a reddish-brown pepper with a strong, pungent aroma and flavor. Its potent flavor has time-delayed action and may not be noticed immediately. It is usually sold whole or crushed in small packages and should be used sparingly. Store it in an airtight container in a cool, dark place for up to 1 year.

Tofu (also called bean curd): puréed soybeans pressed to form a white custardlike cake, used as a vegetable and as an excellent source of protein. Bean curd can be used in all kinds of recipes because it readily absorbs the flavor of other foods. Tofu is available fresh. Store opened tofu submerged in water in a covered container in the refrigerator for up to 3 days. Drain and discard the water and replace it with fresh cold water daily. Tofu may also be stored tightly wrapped in plastic in the refrigerator for a few days.

Water chestnuts: walnut-sized bulbs from an aquatic plant. The bulb has a tough, brown skin and crisp, white interior. Water chestnuts are served separately as a vegetable and are used to add crisp texture and a delicate sweet flavor to dishes. They are available fresh or canned. Store opened, canned water chestnuts in a covered container in the refrigerator for up to 1 week. Store fresh, unpeeled water chestnuts in a plastic bag in the refrigerator for up to 1 week.

Wonton wrappers: commercially prepared thin dough made of flour and water, rolled very thin and cut into 3- and 4-inch squares. They are available fresh or frozen.

Wood ears (also called tree ears or cloud ears): a dried fungus that expands to five or six times its dehydrated size when soaked in warm water. They have a delicate flavor and crunchy texture and are most often used in soups. They are available in cellophane packages.

8

Spicy Chicken **(page 44)**

KIKKOMAN

ORIENTAL COOKING

APPETIZERS

CRISPY WONTONS

¾ pound ground pork
8 water chestnuts, finely chopped
¼ cup finely chopped green onions and
　tops
1 tablespoon Kikkoman Soy Sauce
½ teaspoon salt
1 teaspoon cornstarch
½ teaspoon grated fresh ginger root
1 package (1 lb.) wonton skins
　Vegetable oil for frying
　Tomato catsup and hot mustard *or*
　Kikkoman Sweet & Sour Sauce

Combine pork, water chestnuts, green onions, soy sauce, salt, cornstarch and ginger in medium bowl; mix well. Place ½ teaspoonful pork mixture in center of each wonton skin. Fold wonton skin over filling to form a triangle. Turn top of triangle down to meet fold. Turn over; moisten 1 corner with water. Overlap opposite corner over moistened corner; press firmly. Heat oil in wok or large saucepan over medium-high heat to 375°F. Deep fry wontons, a few at a time, 2 to 3 minutes, or until brown and crispy. Drain on paper towels. Serve warm with catsup and mustard or sweet & sour sauce, as desired.

Makes 10 appetizer servings

EGG DROP SOUP

3 quarts water
9 chicken bouillon cubes
⅓ cup Kikkoman Soy Sauce
6 eggs, well beaten
1½ cups finely chopped green onions and
　tops

Bring water to boil in large saucepan; add bouillon cubes and stir until dissolved. Stir in soy sauce; return to boil. Remove from heat; add eggs all at once, stirring rapidly in 1 direction with spoon. (Eggs will separate to form fine threads.) Stir in green onions. Serve immediately. *Makes about 12 cups*

頭枱食譜

Crispy Wontons

SPICY PORK STRIPS

1 pound boneless pork chops, ½ inch
    thick
⅓ cup Kikkoman Soy Sauce
¼ cup minced green onions and tops
1 tablespoon sugar
1 tablespoon sesame seed, toasted
3 tablespoons water
1½ teaspoons minced fresh ginger root
1 teaspoon Tabasco pepper sauce
1 clove garlic, minced

Slice pork into ¼-inch-thick strips, about 4 inches long. Thread onto metal or bamboo skewers, keeping meat as flat as possible. Arrange skewers in large shallow pan. Blend soy sauce, green onions, sugar, sesame seed, water, ginger, pepper sauce and garlic, stirring until sugar dissolves. Pour mixture evenly over skewers; turn over to coat all sides. Let stand 30 minutes, turning skewers over occasionally. Reserving marinade, remove skewers and place on rack of broiler pan; brush with reserved marinade. Broil 3 minutes, or until pork is tender, turning once and basting with additional marinade. *Makes 6 to 8 appetizer servings*

Left to Right: Beef Kushisashi, Spicy Pork Strips

BEEF KUSHISASHI

½ cup Kikkoman Soy Sauce
¼ cup chopped green onions and tops
2 tablespoons sugar
1 tablespoon vegetable oil
1½ teaspoons cornstarch
1 clove garlic, pressed
1 teaspoon grated fresh ginger root
2½ pounds boneless beef sirloin steak

Blend soy sauce, green onions, sugar, oil, cornstarch, garlic and ginger in small saucepan. Simmer, stirring constantly, until thickened, about 1 minute; cool. Cover and set aside. Slice beef into ⅛-inch-thick strips about 4 inches long and 1 inch wide. Thread onto bamboo or metal skewers keeping meat as flat as possible; brush both sides of beef with sauce. Place skewers on rack of broiler pan; broil to desired degree of doneness.

Makes 10 to 12 appetizer servings

EGG FLOWER SOUP WITH CORN

1 can (10½ oz.) condensed chicken broth
2 soup cans water
2 slices fresh ginger root, each ¼ inch
  thick
2 tablespoons plus 2 teaspoons
  cornstarch
¼ cup water
½ cup whole kernel corn
1 egg, beaten
2 tablespoons chopped green onions and
  tops
4 teaspoons Kikkoman Soy Sauce

Combine chicken broth, 2 soup cans water and ginger in medium saucepan. Bring to boil over high heat; reduce heat, cover and simmer 5 minutes. Discard ginger. Combine cornstarch and ¼ cup water; stir into saucepan with corn. Cook over high heat, stirring constantly, until mixture boils and is slightly thickened. Gradually pour egg into boiling soup, stirring constantly, but gently, in 1 direction. Remove from heat; stir in green onions and soy sauce. Serve immediately. *Makes about 4½ cups*

YAKITORI

3 pounds chicken breasts
1 bunch green onions, cut into 1-inch
  lengths
1 pound chicken livers, trimmed, rinsed
  and drained
1 cup Kikkoman Soy Sauce
¼ cup sugar
1 tablespoon vegetable oil
2 cloves garlic, pressed
¾ teaspoon ground ginger

Remove skin and bones from chicken, keeping meat in 1 piece; cut into 1-inch lengths. Thread chicken pieces onto metal or bamboo skewers with green onions (spear through side) and chicken livers. Arrange skewers in large shallow pan. Blend soy sauce, sugar, oil, garlic and ginger; pour mixture over skewers. Brush each skewer thoroughly with sauce. Cover and refrigerate about 1 hour, turning skewers over occasionally. Reserving marinade, remove skewers and place on rack of broiler pan. Broil 5 inches from heat source 3 minutes on each side, or until chicken is tender; brush with reserved marinade after turning. *Makes 4 dozen appetizers*

EMPRESS CHICKEN WINGS

1½ pounds chicken wings (about 8 wings)
3 tablespoons Kikkoman Soy Sauce
1 tablespoon dry sherry
1 tablespoon minced fresh ginger root
1 clove garlic, minced
2 tablespoons vegetable oil
¼ to ⅓ cup cornstarch
⅔ cup water
2 green onions and tops, cut diagonally
    into thin slices
1 teaspoon slivered fresh ginger root

Disjoint chicken wings; discard tips (or save for stock). Combine soy sauce, sherry, minced ginger and garlic in large bowl; stir in chicken. Cover and refrigerate 1 hour, stirring occasionally. Remove chicken; reserve marinade. Heat oil in large skillet over medium heat. Lightly coat chicken pieces with cornstarch; add to skillet and brown slowly on all sides. Remove chicken; drain off fat. Stir water and reserved marinade into same skillet. Add chicken; sprinkle green onions and slivered ginger evenly over chicken. Cover and simmer 5 minutes, or until chicken is tender.   *Makes 4 to 6 appetizer servings*

SHRIMP TERIYAKI

½ cup Kikkoman Soy Sauce
2 tablespoons sugar
1 tablespoon vegetable oil
1½ teaspoons cornstarch
1 clove garlic, crushed
1 teaspoon minced fresh ginger root
2 tablespoons water
2 pounds medium-size raw shrimp, peeled
    and deveined

Blend soy sauce, sugar, oil, cornstarch, garlic, ginger and water in small saucepan. Simmer, stirring constantly, until thickened, about 1 minute; cool. Coat shrimp with sauce; drain off excess. Place on rack of broiler pan. Broil 5 inches from heat source 3 to 4 minutes on each side, or until shrimp are opaque and cooked. Serve immediately with wooden picks.

Makes 10 appetizer servings

CANTONESE MEATBALLS

1 can (20 oz.) pineapple chunks in syrup
3 tablespoons brown sugar, packed
5 tablespoons Kikkoman Teriyaki Sauce,
    divided
1 tablespoon vinegar
1 tablespoon tomato catsup
1 pound lean ground beef
2 tablespoons instant minced onion
2 tablespoons cornstarch
¼ cup water

Drain pineapple; reserve syrup. Combine syrup, brown sugar, 3 tablespoons teriyaki sauce, vinegar and catsup; set aside. Mix beef with remaining 2 tablespoons teriyaki sauce and onion; shape into 20 meatballs. Brown meatballs in large skillet; drain off excess fat. Pour syrup mixture over meatballs; simmer 10 minutes, stirring occasionally. Dissolve cornstarch in water; stir into skillet with pineapple. Cook and stir until sauce thickens and pineapple is heated through.   *Makes 6 to 8 appetizer servings*

Empress Chicken Wings

Prawns-in-Shell

PRAWNS-IN-SHELL

1 pound large raw prawns
2 tablespoons dry white wine, divided
½ teaspoon grated fresh ginger root
¼ cup vegetable oil
2 tablespoons coarsely chopped green
    onions and tops
1 teaspoon coarsely chopped fresh ginger
    root
1 clove garlic, chopped
2 small red chili peppers,* coarsely
    chopped
1 tablespoon sugar
3 tablespoons tomato catsup
2 tablespoons Kikkoman Soy Sauce
½ teaspoon cornstarch

Wash and devein prawns; do not peel. Cut prawns diagonally into halves; place in medium bowl. Sprinkle 1 tablespoon wine and grated ginger over prawns. Heat oil in hot wok or large skillet over high heat. Add prawns; stir-fry until completely pink or red. Add green onions, chopped ginger, garlic and chili peppers; stir-fry only until onions are tender. Combine sugar, catsup, soy sauce, remaining 1 tablespoon wine and cornstarch; pour into pan. Cook and stir until sauce boils and thickens. Serve immediately. Garnish as desired. *Makes 8 appetizer servings*

*Wear rubber gloves when working with chilis and wash hands in warm soapy water. Avoid touching face or eyes.

SESAME CHEESE CRACKERS

1 cup all-purpose flour
½ teaspoon salt
⅛ teaspoon ground red pepper (cayenne)
6 tablespoons cold butter or margarine
1 cup (4 oz.) finely grated Cheddar cheese
¼ cup sesame seed, toasted
½ teaspoon Kikkoman Soy Sauce
4½ to 7½ teaspoons ice-cold water

Combine flour, salt and pepper in medium bowl; cut in butter until mixture resembles coarse crumbs. Stir in cheese and sesame seed. Combine soy sauce and 3 teaspoons water; stir into dry ingredients. Add more water, a little at a time, mixing lightly until dough begins to stick together. Turn out dough and press together on lightly floured board or pastry cloth; roll out to ⅛-inch thickness. Cut dough into 2×1-inch rectangles with pastry wheel or knife. Place on lightly greased baking sheets and bake at 400°F. 8 to 10 minutes, or until lightly browned. Remove crackers to rack to cool. *Makes 8 appetizer servings*

BITS O' TERIYAKI CHICKEN

½ cup Kikkoman Teriyaki Sauce
1 teaspoon sugar
2 whole chicken breasts, skinned and
    boned
1 teaspoon cornstarch
1 tablespoon water
1 tablespoon vegetable oil
2 tablespoons sesame seed, toasted

Combine teriyaki sauce and sugar in small bowl. Cut chicken into 1-inch pieces; stir into teriyaki sauce mixture. Marinate 30 minutes, stirring occasionally. Remove chicken; reserve 2 tablespoons marinade. Combine reserved marinade, cornstarch and water in small bowl; set aside. Heat oil in hot wok or large skillet over medium-high heat. Add chicken and sesame seed; stir-fry 2 minutes. Stir in cornstarch mixture. Cook and stir until mixture boils and thickens and chicken is tender, about 1 minute. Turn into chafing dish or onto serving platter. Serve warm with wooden picks. *Makes 6 appetizer servings*

STEAMED STUFFED ZUCCHINI ROUNDS

4 zucchini, 6 to 7 inches long, about
    1½ inches in diameter
½ cup Kikkoman Teriyaki Sauce
½ pound ground beef
½ cup dry bread crumbs
¼ cup minced green onions and tops

Trim off and discard ends of zucchini; cut crosswise into ¾-inch lengths. Scoop out flesh, leaving about ⅛-inch shell on sides and bottoms; reserve flesh. Place zucchini rounds in large plastic bag; pour in teriyaki sauce. Press air out of bag; tie top securely. Marinate 30 minutes, turning bag over occasionally. Meanwhile, coarsely chop zucchini flesh; reserve ½ cup. Remove zucchini rounds from marinade; reserve ¼ cup marinade. Combine reserved marinade with beef, bread crumbs, green onions and ½ cup reserved zucchini flesh. Fill each round with about 2 teaspoonfuls beef mixture. Place rounds, filled side up, on steamer rack. Set rack in large pot or wok of boiling water. (Do not allow water level to reach zucchini.) Cover and steam 6 minutes, or until zucchini rounds are tender-crisp when pierced with fork. Serve immediately.   *Makes 6 to 8 appetizer servings*

WAIKIKI APPETIZERS

1½ pounds bulk pork sausage
1 can (20 oz.) pineapple chunks in syrup
½ cup brown sugar, packed
¼ cup lemon juice
2 tablespoons cornstarch
2 tablespoons Kikkoman Soy Sauce
½ cup chopped green pepper
½ cup drained maraschino cherries

Shape sausage into ½- to ¾-inch balls. Place in single layer in baking pan. Bake in 400°F. oven 25 minutes, or until cooked; drain on paper towels. Meanwhile, drain pineapple; reserve syrup. Add enough water to syrup to measure 1 cup; combine with brown sugar, lemon juice, cornstarch and soy sauce in large saucepan. Cook and stir until sauce boils and thickens. Fold in green pepper, cherries, pineapple chunks and drained cooked sausage. To serve, turn into chafing dish.   *Makes 6 to 8 appetizer servings*

HUNAN–STYLE STUFFED CUCUMBERS

3 cucumbers, each about 6 inches long
¼ pound medium-size raw shrimp, peeled
    and deveined
¾ pound ground pork
2 tablespoons Kikkoman Soy Sauce
2 tablespoons finely chopped green onion
    and tops
¼ to ½ teaspoon crushed red pepper
1 clove garlic, pressed

Trim off and discard ends of cucumbers, then peel lengthwise with vegetable peeler to form stripes. Cut each cucumber crosswise into 1½-inch lengths. Scoop out and discard seeds and enough flesh to make about ¼-inch shell on sides and bottoms; set aside. Mince shrimp; combine with pork, soy sauce, green onion, red pepper and garlic. Stuff cucumber shells evenly with mixture; place on steamer rack. Set rack in large pot or wok of boiling water. (Do not allow water level to reach cucumbers.) Cover and steam 12 to 15 minutes, or until pork is cooked.   *Makes 4 to 6 appetizer servings*

Top to Bottom: Steamed Stuffed Zucchini Rounds,
Waikiki Appetizers

Glazed Ginger Chicken

GLAZED GINGER CHICKEN

1 tablespoon sesame seed, toasted
1 tablespoon cornstarch
5 tablespoons Kikkoman Soy Sauce
3 tablespoons plum jam
1 tablespoon minced fresh ginger root
1 clove garlic, pressed
8 small chicken thighs (about 2 pounds)

Cut eight 8-inch squares of aluminum foil; set aside. Combine sesame seed, cornstarch, soy sauce, plum jam, ginger and garlic in small saucepan. Bring to boil over medium heat, stirring constantly. Remove from heat and cool slightly. Stir in thighs, a few at a time, to coat each piece well. Place 1 thigh, skin side up, on each foil square. Divide and spoon remaining sauce evenly over thighs. Fold ends of foil to form a package; crease and fold down to secure well. Place foil bundles, seam side up, in single layer, on steamer rack. Set rack in large pot or wok of boiling water. (Do not allow water level to reach bundles.) Cover and steam 30 minutes, or until chicken is tender. Garnish as desired. Serve immediately. *Makes 8 appetizer servings*

SPRING ROLLS

½ pound ground pork
1 teaspoon Kikkoman Soy Sauce
1 teaspoon dry sherry
½ teaspoon garlic salt
2 tablespoons vegetable oil
3 cups fresh bean sprouts
½ cup sliced onion
1 tablespoon Kikkoman Soy Sauce
1 tablespoon cornstarch
¾ cup water, divided
8 sheets egg roll skins
½ cup prepared biscuit mix
1 egg, beaten
　Vegetable oil for frying
　Hot mustard, tomato catsup and
　　Kikkoman Soy Sauce

Combine pork, 1 teaspoon soy sauce, sherry and garlic salt; mix well. Let stand 15 minutes. Heat 2 tablespoons oil in hot wok or large skillet over medium-high heat; brown pork mixture in hot oil. Add bean sprouts, onion and 1 tablespoon soy sauce. Stir-fry until vegetables are tender-crisp; drain and cool. Dissolve cornstarch in ¼ cup water. Place about ⅓ cupful pork mixture on lower half of egg roll skin. Moisten left and right edges with cornstarch mixture. Fold bottom edge up to just cover filling. Fold left and right edges ½ inch over; roll up jelly-roll fashion. Moisten top edge with cornstarch mixture and seal. Complete all rolls. Combine biscuit mix, egg and remaining ½ cup water in small bowl; dip each roll in batter. Heat oil for frying in wok or large saucepan over medium-high heat to 370°F. Deep fry rolls, a few at a time, in hot oil 5 to 7 minutes, or until golden brown, turning often. Drain on paper towels. Slice each roll into 4 pieces. Serve with mustard, catsup and soy sauce as desired.

Makes 8 appetizer servings

MEAT−FILLED ORIENTAL PANCAKES

6 Oriental Pancakes (recipe follows)
1 tablespoon cornstarch
3 tablespoons Kikkoman Soy Sauce
1 tablespoon dry sherry
¾ pound ground beef
½ pound ground pork
⅔ cup chopped green onions and tops
1 teaspoon minced fresh ginger root
1 clove garlic, pressed

Prepare Oriental Pancakes. Combine cornstarch, soy sauce and sherry in large bowl. Add beef, pork, green onions, ginger and garlic; mix until thoroughly combined. Spread ½ cup meat mixture evenly over each pancake, leaving about a ½-inch border on 1 side. Starting with opposite side, roll up pancake jelly-roll fashion. Place rolls, seam side down, in single layer, on heatproof plate; place plate on steamer rack. Set rack in large pot or wok of boiling water. Cover and steam 15 minutes. (For best results, steam all rolls at the same time.) Just before serving, cut rolls diagonally into quarters. Arrange on serving platter and serve hot.

Makes 2 dozen appetizers

ORIENTAL PANCAKES

Beat *4 eggs* in large bowl with wire whisk. Combine *½ cup water, 3 tablespoons cornstarch, 2 teaspoons Kikkoman Soy Sauce* and *½ teaspoon sugar;* pour into eggs and beat well. Heat an 8-inch omelet or crêpe pan over medium heat. Brush bottom of pan with *½ teaspoon vegetable oil;* reduce heat to low. Beat egg mixture; pour ¼ cupful into skillet, lifting and tipping pan from side to side to form a thin round pancake. Cook about 1 to 1½ minutes, or until firm. Carefully lift with spatula and transfer to a sheet of waxed paper. Continue procedure, adding *½ teaspoon oil* to pan for each pancake.

Makes 6 pancakes

SAUCY SHRIMP

½ pound medium-size raw shrimp
¼ cup Kikkoman Teriyaki Baste & Glaze
2 tablespoons dry sherry
1 tablespoon lime juice
1 tablespoon sliced green onions and tops
3 to 4 drops Tabasco pepper sauce

Peel, devein and butterfly shrimp. Combine teriyaki baste & glaze, sherry, lime juice, green onions and pepper sauce in medium bowl; stir in shrimp. Cover; refrigerate at least 1 hour, stirring occasionally. Remove shrimp and place on rack of broiler pan. Broil 2 to 3 minutes on each side, or until shrimp are opaque and cooked. Serve immediately with wooden picks.

Makes 6 appetizer servings

Meat-Filled Oriental Pancakes

Drums of Heaven

DRUMS OF HEAVEN

   1 tablespoon Kikkoman Soy Sauce
   1 tablespoon dry sherry
 18 chicken wing drumettes
   ⅓ cup Kikkoman Teriyaki Baste & Glaze
   1 large clove garlic, pressed
   2 teaspoons sesame seed, toasted

Combine soy sauce and sherry in large bowl; stir in drumettes until well coated. Arrange drumettes, side by side, on large rack in shallow foil-lined baking pan. Bake in 425°F. oven 30 minutes. Meanwhile, mix teriyaki baste & glaze and garlic; brush tops of drumettes with half of glaze. Turn pieces over and brush with remaining glaze. Bake 15 minutes longer, or until drumettes are tender; sprinkle with sesame seed.

Makes 6 appetizer servings

PARCHMENT—WRAPPED CHICKEN

2 whole chicken breasts, skinned and
    boned
3 tablespoons Kikkoman Soy Sauce
1 teaspoon ginger juice*
¼ teaspoon sugar
    Boiling water
½ pound fresh bean sprouts
6 green onions and tops, cut into 2-inch
    lengths and slivered
⅓ cup chopped toasted walnuts

Cut eight 8-inch squares of parchment paper; set aside. Cut chicken into thin, narrow strips, about 3 inches long. Combine soy sauce, ginger juice and sugar in large bowl; stir in chicken. Let stand 30 minutes. Meanwhile, pour boiling water over bean sprouts; let stand 1 minute. Drain; cool under cold water and drain well. Thoroughly toss chicken mixture with bean sprouts, green onions and walnuts. Place about ½ cupful chicken mixture in center of each parchment square. Fold bottom point of parchment over filling; crease just below filling and fold point over and under filling. Fold side points over filling, overlapping slightly. Crease paper to hold folds. Fold remaining corner down so point extends below bottom of bundle; tuck this point between folded sides. Crease paper to hold folds. Repeat with remaining parchment squares. Place bundles, seam side down, in single layer, on steamer rack. Set rack in large pot or wok of boiling water. (Do not allow water level to reach bundles.) Cover and steam about 7 minutes, or until chicken is tender. Serve immediately. *Makes 8 appetizer servings*

*Peel fresh ginger root, then squeeze through garlic press.

MONGOLIAN ALMONDS

1 cup whole natural almonds
2 tablespoons Kikkoman Teriyaki Sauce
1 teaspoon brown sugar
⅛ to ¼ teaspoon Tabasco pepper sauce
1 tablespoon water
½ teaspoon vegetable oil

Toast almonds on ungreased baking sheet in preheated 350°F. oven 10 minutes without stirring. Remove pan from oven and cool almonds in pan on wire rack. *Reduce oven temperature to 250°F.* Combine teriyaki sauce, brown sugar, pepper sauce and water in narrow 1-quart saucepan. Bring to boil over medium-low heat. Stir in almonds and boil about 5 minutes, or until sauce is absorbed by almonds, stirring frequently. Add oil and toss almonds until coated; turn out onto baking sheet, separating almonds. Bake 5 minutes; stir and turn almonds over. Bake 5 minutes longer. Remove almonds from pan to large plate; cool in single layer. Store in loose-fitting container or plastic bag.

Makes 1 cup

MEATS

SZECHUAN BEEF & SNOW PEAS

½ pound boneless tender beef steak
    (sirloin, rib eye or top loin)
2 tablespoons cornstarch, divided
3 tablespoons Kikkoman Soy Sauce,
    divided
1 tablespoon dry sherry
1 clove garlic, minced
¾ cup water
¼ to ½ teaspoon crushed red pepper
2 tablespoons vegetable oil, divided
6 ounces fresh snow peas, trimmed
1 medium onion, chunked
    Salt
1 medium tomato, chunked
    Hot cooked rice

Slice beef across grain into thin strips. Combine 1 tablespoon *each* cornstarch and soy sauce with sherry and garlic in small bowl; stir in beef. Let stand 15 minutes. Meanwhile, combine water, remaining 1 tablespoon cornstarch, 2 tablespoons soy sauce and red pepper; set aside. Heat 1 tablespoon oil in hot wok or large skillet over high heat. Add beef and stir-fry 1 minute; remove. Heat remaining 1 tablespoon oil in same pan. Add snow peas and onion; lightly sprinkle with salt and stir-fry 3 minutes. Add beef, soy sauce mixture and tomato. Cook and stir until sauce boils and thickens and tomato is heated through. Serve immediately with rice. *Makes 2 to 3 servings*

SPARERIBS CHINESE

4 pounds pork spareribs
½ cup Kikkoman Soy Sauce
⅓ cup honey
¼ cup dry sherry
1 clove garlic, pressed
¼ teaspoon ground ginger

Cut ribs into serving pieces; place, meaty-side down, in shallow, foil-lined baking pan. Combine soy sauce, honey, sherry, garlic and ginger; brush ribs thoroughly with sauce. Cover pan loosely with foil and bake in 350°F. oven 1 hour. Uncover; turn ribs over. Pour remaining sauce over ribs and brush thoroughly. Bake, uncovered, 30 minutes longer, or until ribs are tender, brushing with sauce occasionally. *Makes 4 to 6 servings*

肉類食譜

Szechuan Beef & Snow Peas

FIERY BEEF STIR-FRY

½ pound boneless tender beef steak
   (sirloin, rib eye or top loin)
1 tablespoon cornstarch
4 tablespoons Kikkoman Soy Sauce,
   divided
½ teaspoon sugar
1 clove garlic, minced
1¼ cups water
4 teaspoons cornstarch
1½ teaspoons distilled white vinegar
⅛ to ¼ teaspoon ground red pepper
   (cayenne)
3 tablespoons vegetable oil, divided
3 cups bite-size cauliflowerets
   Salt
1 onion, chunked and separated
1 green pepper, chunked

Cut beef across grain into thin strips. Combine 1 tablespoon *each* cornstarch and soy sauce with sugar and garlic in small bowl; stir in beef. Let stand 15 minutes. Meanwhile, combine water, remaining 3 tablespoons soy sauce, 4 teaspoons cornstarch, vinegar and red pepper; set aside. Heat 1 tablespoon oil in hot wok or large skillet over high heat. Add beef and stir-fry 1 minute; remove. Heat remaining 2 tablespoons oil in same pan. Add cauliflowerets; lightly sprinkle with salt and stir-fry 2 minutes. Add onion and green pepper; stir-fry 4 minutes. Stir in beef and soy sauce mixture; cook and stir until sauce boils and thickens. *Makes 2 to 3 servings*

HUNAN STIR-FRY WITH TOFU

1 block tofu
½ pound ground pork
1 tablespoon dry sherry
1 teaspoon minced fresh ginger root
1 clove garlic, minced
½ cup regular-strength chicken broth
1 tablespoon cornstarch
3 tablespoons Kikkoman Soy Sauce
1 tablespoon vinegar
½ teaspoon crushed red pepper
1 tablespoon vegetable oil
1 onion, cut into ¾-inch pieces
1 green pepper, cut into ¾-inch pieces
   Hot cooked rice

Cut tofu into ½-inch cubes; drain well on several layers of paper towels. Meanwhile, combine pork, sherry, ginger and garlic in small bowl; let stand 10 minutes. Blend broth, cornstarch, soy sauce, vinegar and red pepper; set aside. Heat wok or large skillet over medium-high heat; add pork. Cook, stirring to separate pork, about 3 minutes, or until lightly browned; remove. Heat oil in same pan. Add onion and green pepper; stir-fry 4 minutes. Add pork and soy sauce mixture. Cook and stir until mixture boils and thickens. Gently fold in tofu; heat through. Serve immediately over rice. *Makes 4 servings*

ORIENTAL PORK BUNDLES

Plum Sauce (recipe follows)
⅓ cup Kikkoman Stir-Fry Sauce
1 clove garlic, pressed
½ pound boneless lean pork, diced
½ teaspoon vegetable oil
2 eggs, beaten
2 tablespoons vegetable oil, divided
2 stalks celery, diced
1 medium carrot, diced
1 small onion, diced
2 ounces fresh mushrooms, coarsely chopped
6 (8-inch) flour tortillas, warmed
3 cups finely shredded iceberg lettuce

Prepare Plum Sauce; cool while preparing filling. Combine stir-fry sauce and garlic. Coat pork with 1 tablespoon stir-fry sauce mixture; let stand 10 minutes. Meanwhile, heat ½ teaspoon oil in hot wok or large skillet over medium-high heat. Pour in eggs and scramble; remove. Heat 1 tablespoon oil in same pan. Add pork and stir-fry 3 minutes; remove. Heat remaining 1 tablespoon oil in same pan. Add celery, carrot, onion and mushrooms; stir-fry 4 minutes. Stir in eggs, pork and remaining stir-fry sauce mixture. Cook and stir just until pork and vegetables are coated with sauce. Spread 1 tablespoon Plum Sauce on each tortilla; top with desired amount of shredded lettuce and pork mixture. Wrap or fold over to enclose filling. *Makes 4 to 6 servings*

PLUM SAUCE

Combine *¼ cup plum jam, 2 tablespoons Kikkoman Stir-Fry Sauce* and *½ teaspoon distilled white vinegar* in small saucepan. Cook, stirring constantly, over medium-high heat until mixture comes to a boil and is smooth.

Oriental Pork Bundles

Colorful Stir-Fried Pork

COLORFUL STIR-FRIED PORK

⅓ cup Kikkoman Stir-Fry Sauce
1 teaspoon distilled white vinegar
¼ to ½ teaspoon crushed red pepper
¾ pound boneless lean pork
1 tablespoon Kikkoman Stir-Fry Sauce
3 tablespoons vegetable oil, divided
2 medium carrots, cut into julienne strips
1 medium onion, halved and sliced
¼ pound fresh snow peas, trimmed and
    cut lengthwise in half

Combine ⅓ cup stir-fry sauce, vinegar and red pepper; set aside. Cut pork across grain into thin slices, then into strips; coat with 1 tablespoon stir-fry sauce. Heat 1 tablespoon oil in hot wok or large skillet over high heat. Add pork and stir-fry 2 minutes; remove. Heat remaining 2 tablespoons oil in same pan. Add carrots, onion and snow peas; stir-fry 4 minutes. Stir in pork and stir-fry sauce mixture. Cook and stir just until pork and vegetables are coated with sauce. Serve immediately.   *Makes 4 servings*

SZECHUAN BEEF STEW

2 pounds boneless beef chuck
2 cloves garlic, pressed
4 tablespoons Kikkoman Soy Sauce,
    divided
3 teaspoons sugar, divided
1 cup water
½ to ¾ teaspoon crushed red pepper
¾ teaspoon fennel seed, crushed
¼ teaspoon black pepper
¼ teaspoon ground cloves
¼ teaspoon ground ginger
1 tablespoon vegetable oil
2 tablespoons cornstarch
2 tablespoons water

Cut beef into 2-inch cubes. Combine garlic, 2 tablespoons soy sauce and 1 teaspoon sugar in large bowl; stir in beef cubes until well coated. Let stand 15 minutes. Meanwhile, combine 1 cup water, remaining 2 tablespoons soy sauce, 2 teaspoons sugar, red pepper, fennel, black pepper, cloves and ginger; set aside. Heat oil in Dutch oven or large skillet over high heat. Brown beef on all sides in hot oil. Stir in soy sauce mixture. Bring to boil; reduce heat and simmer, covered, 2 hours, or until beef is very tender. Combine cornstarch with 2 tablespoons water; stir into beef mixture. Cook and stir until mixture boils and thickens, about 1 minute.   *Makes 6 servings*

SIMPLY SUPER SUKIYAKI

1 block tofu
½ cup Kikkoman Soy Sauce
½ cup water
2 tablespoons sugar
¾ pound ground beef
1 medium-size yellow onion, thinly sliced
1 pound fresh spinach, trimmed, washed
    and drained
1 bunch green onions, cut into 2-inch
    lengths, separating whites from tops
¼ pound fresh mushrooms, sliced

Cut tofu into 1-inch cubes; drain well on several layers of paper towels. Meanwhile, combine soy sauce, water and sugar; set aside. Brown beef in Dutch oven or large skillet over medium heat, stirring to break beef into large chunks. Add yellow onion; cook 1 minute. Add spinach, white parts of green onions, mushrooms and soy sauce mixture; cook until spinach wilts, stirring constantly. Gently stir in tofu and green onion tops. Cook 5 to 7 minutes, or until vegetables are tender and tofu is seasoned with sauce.   *Makes 4 to 6 servings*

CELEBRATION PORK & RICE

¾ pound boneless lean pork
6 tablespoons Kikkoman Stir-Fry Sauce,
    divided
⅛ to ¼ teaspoon pepper
2 tablespoons vegetable oil, divided
1½ cups frozen peas & carrots, thawed
½ cup chopped onion
⅛ teaspoon salt
3½ cups cold cooked rice

Cut pork across grain into thin slices, then into slivers; combine with 2 tablespoons stir-fry sauce. Stir pepper into remaining 4 tablespoons stir-fry sauce; set aside. Heat 1 tablespoon oil in hot wok or large skillet over high heat. Add pork and stir-fry 3 minutes; remove. Heat remaining 1 tablespoon oil in same pan. Add peas & carrots, onion and salt; stir-fry 2 minutes. Remove from heat and gently stir in rice to combine. Return to medium-high heat; stir in pork and stir-fry sauce mixture. Cook and stir until rice is thoroughly heated and coated with sauce. *Makes 4 servings*

DRAGON BEEF KABOBS

1¼ pounds boneless beef sirloin steak,
    1½ inches thick
¼ cup Kikkoman Teriyaki Sauce
1 tablespoon peanut butter
1 teaspoon brown sugar
1 teaspoon garlic powder
½ teaspoon Tabasco pepper sauce
1 can (8¼ oz.) pineapple chunks, drained

MICROWAVE DIRECTIONS: Cut beef into 1½-inch cubes; place in medium bowl. Blend teriyaki sauce, peanut butter, brown sugar, garlic powder and pepper sauce. Pour mixture over beef, turning pieces over to coat thoroughly. Marinate 1 hour, turning pieces over occasionally. Reserving marinade, remove beef and thread alternately with pineapple chunks on 4 wooden or bamboo skewers. Arrange skewers in single layer on 12-inch round microwave-safe platter. Brush with reserved marinade. Microwave on High 2 minutes. Turn skewers over and rotate positions on platter, moving center skewers to edge. Brush with marinade. Microwave on High 2 minutes longer, or to desired degree of doneness. *Makes 4 servings*

CANTONESE STIR-FRY

¾ pound boneless beef sirloin, lean pork
    or chicken
1 tablespoon Kikkoman Stir-Fry Sauce
2 tablespoons vegetable oil, divided
2 small zucchini, cut crosswise into
    ¼-inch-thick slices
1 onion, chunked
12 cherry tomatoes, halved
¼ cup Kikkoman Stir-Fry Sauce

Cut beef, pork or chicken across grain into thin slices, then into slivers; coat with 1 tablespoon stir-fry sauce. Heat 1 tablespoon oil in hot wok or large skillet over high heat. Add beef and stir-fry 1 minute (stir-fry pork or chicken 2 minutes); remove. Heat remaining 1 tablespoon oil in same pan. Add zucchini and onion; stir-fry 4 minutes. Stir in beef, tomatoes and ¼ cup stir-fry sauce. Cook and stir until beef and vegetables are coated with sauce and tomatoes are heated through. Serve immediately. *Makes 4 servings*

Classic Chinese Pepper Steak

CLASSIC CHINESE PEPPER STEAK

1 pound boneless beef sirloin steak
1 tablespoon Kikkoman Stir-Fry Sauce
2 tablespoons vegetable oil, divided
2 medium-size green, red or yellow bell
    peppers, cut into 1-inch squares
2 medium onions, cut into 1-inch squares
¼ cup Kikkoman Stir-Fry Sauce
    Hot cooked rice (optional)

Cut beef across grain into thin strips, then into 1-inch squares; coat with 1 tablespoon stir-fry sauce. Heat 1 tablespoon oil in hot wok or large skillet over high heat. Add beef and stir-fry 1 minute; remove. Heat remaining 1 tablespoon oil in same pan. Add peppers and onions; stir-fry 5 minutes. Stir in beef and ¼ cup stir-fry sauce; cook and stir just until beef and vegetables are coated with sauce. Serve immediately with rice.

Makes 4 servings

STIR-FRY LAMB WITH FLOWER BUNS

Flower Buns (recipe follows)
¾ pound boneless lamb leg or shoulder
4 tablespoons Kikkoman Soy Sauce, divided
2 tablespoons cornstarch, divided
1 clove garlic, minced
¼ cup water
3 tablespoons vegetable oil, divided
1 teaspoon minced fresh ginger root
½ pound fresh bean sprouts
¼ pound fresh snow peas, trimmed and cut into julienne strips
2 medium carrots, cut into julienne strips

Prepare Flower Buns. Cut lamb into thin strips. Combine 1 tablespoon *each* soy sauce and cornstarch with garlic in medium bowl; stir in lamb. Let stand 10 minutes. Meanwhile, combine remaining 3 tablespoons soy sauce, 1 tablespoon cornstarch and water; set aside. Heat 1 tablespoon oil in hot wok or large skillet over high heat. Add lamb and stir-fry 1 minute; remove. Heat remaining 2 tablespoons oil in same pan. Add ginger; stir-fry 30 seconds. Add bean sprouts, snow peas and carrots; stir-fry 2 minutes. Add lamb and soy sauce mixture. Cook and stir until sauce boils and thickens. Serve immediately with Flower Buns.
Makes 4 to 6 servings

FLOWER BUNS

2 cups quick biscuit mix
2 tablespoons chopped green onion and tops
1 tablespoon sugar
⅓ cup plus 1 tablespoon water
All-purpose flour
Vegetable oil

Combine quick biscuit mix, green onion and sugar. Add water all at once; stir to form a soft dough. Turn out onto lightly floured surface; knead gently 30 seconds. Divide dough in half; roll out half of dough to 9-inch square. Brush lightly with vegetable oil, leaving a 1-inch border at top edge. Starting at bottom edge, roll up dough, jelly-roll fashion; seal edge. Cut roll crosswise into 6 equal slices. Firmly press center of each slice, parallel to cut edges, with chopstick. Place on greased steamer rack; set wire rack in large saucepan or wok of boiling water. (Do not allow water level to reach buns.) Cover and steam 12 minutes. Remove to rack placed over cake pan and keep warm in 200°F. oven. Repeat procedure with remaining dough.
Makes 12 buns

BAKE & GLAZE TERI RIBS

3 pounds pork spareribs
½ teaspoon garlic powder
½ teaspoon pepper
⅔ cup Kikkoman Teriyaki Baste & Glaze
½ teaspoon grated lemon peel

Cut ribs into serving pieces; place, meaty side up, in shallow foil-lined baking pan. Sprinkle garlic powder and pepper evenly over ribs; cover pan loosely with foil. Bake in 350°F. oven 45 minutes. Meanwhile, combine teriyaki baste & glaze and lemon peel. Remove foil and brush both sides of ribs with baste & glaze mixture. Cover and bake 40 minutes longer, or until ribs are tender, brushing with baste & glaze mixture occasionally.
Makes 4 servings

Stir-Fry Lamb with Flower Buns

Pork and Peanut Stir-Fry

PORK AND PEANUT STIR-FRY

¼ pound boneless lean pork
4 teaspoons cornstarch, divided
3 tablespoons Kikkoman Lite Soy Sauce,
  divided
1 teaspoon minced fresh ginger root
½ cup water
2 teaspoons distilled white vinegar
¼ teaspoon garlic powder
2 tablespoons vegetable oil, divided
1 medium onion, sliced
1 medium carrot, cut diagonally into
  ⅛-inch-thick slices
2 medium zucchini, cut diagonally into
  ⅛-inch-thick slices
⅓ cup unsalted roasted peanuts
  Hot cooked rice (optional)

Cut pork across grain into thin slices, then into strips. Combine 2 teaspoons *each* cornstarch and lite soy sauce with ginger in small bowl; stir in pork. Let stand 15 minutes. Meanwhile, combine water, remaining 2 teaspoons cornstarch, 2 tablespoons plus 1 teaspoon lite soy sauce, vinegar and garlic powder; set aside. Heat 1 tablespoon oil in hot wok or large skillet over high heat. Add pork and stir-fry 2 minutes; remove. Heat remaining 1 tablespoon oil in same pan. Add onion and carrot; stir-fry 2 minutes. Add zucchini; stir-fry 2 minutes. Stir in pork and soy sauce mixture. Cook and stir until mixture boils and thickens. Stir in peanuts; serve immediately with rice. *Makes 2 to 3 servings*

MONGOLIAN LAMB

1 pound boneless lamb leg or shoulder
3 tablespoons Kikkoman Soy Sauce, divided
1 tablespoon cornstarch
2 cloves garlic, pressed
¾ cup water
2½ teaspoons cornstarch
1 teaspoon sesame seed, toasted
½ teaspoon sugar
⅛ to ¼ teaspoon crushed red pepper
2 tablespoons vegetable oil, divided
2 medium carrots, cut diagonally into thin slices
1 bunch green onions, cut into 2-inch lengths, separating whites from tops
Hot cooked rice

Cut lamb across grain into long, thin slices. Combine 1 tablespoon *each* soy sauce and cornstarch with garlic in medium bowl; stir in lamb. Let stand 10 minutes. Meanwhile, combine water, remaining 2 tablespoons soy sauce, 2½ teaspoons cornstarch, sesame seed, sugar and red pepper; set aside. Heat 1 tablespoon oil in hot wok or large skillet over high heat. Add lamb and stir-fry 1 minute; remove. Heat remaining 1 tablespoon oil in same pan. Add carrots and white parts of green onions; stir-fry 2 minutes. Add green onion tops; stir-fry 1 minute. Add lamb and soy sauce mixture. Cook and stir until sauce boils and thickens. Serve immediately with rice. *Makes 6 servings*

CRISPY LITE SPARERIBS

4 pounds pork spareribs, sawed into thirds across bones
¼ cup Kikkoman Lite Soy Sauce
2 tablespoons dry sherry
1 clove garlic, pressed
Mandarin Peach Sauce (recipe follows)

Cut ribs into 1-rib pieces. Place in steamer basket or on steamer rack. Set basket in large pot or wok of boiling water. (Do not allow water level to reach ribs.) Cover and steam 30 minutes. Meanwhile, combine lite soy sauce, sherry and garlic in large bowl; add ribs and stir to coat each piece well. Marinate 1 hour, stirring frequently. Remove ribs and place, meaty side up, on rack of broiler pan. Bake in 425°F. oven 15 minutes, or until crispy. Serve with warm Mandarin Peach Sauce.

Makes 4 to 6 servings

MANDARIN PEACH SAUCE

Drain *1 can (16 oz.) cling peach slices in juice or extra light syrup;* reserve liquid for another use. Place peaches in blender container. Process on high speed until smooth; pour into small saucepan. Combine *3 tablespoons Kikkoman Teriyaki Sauce* and *1 tablespoon cornstarch;* stir into peaches with *1 tablespoon sugar, ¼ teaspoon fennel seed, crushed, ¼ teaspoon pepper* and *⅛ teaspoon ground cloves*. Bring mixture to boil over medium heat. Simmer until sauce thickens, about 2 minutes, stirring constantly. Remove from heat and stir in *⅛ teaspoon garlic powder*. *Makes 1 cup*

Beef & Napa with Noodles

BEEF & NAPA WITH NOODLES

1 small head napa (Chinese cabbage)
   Boiling water
½ pound boneless tender beef steak
   (sirloin, rib eye or top loin)
6 tablespoons Kikkoman Stir-Fry Sauce,
   divided
⅛ to ¼ teaspoon crushed red pepper
2 tablespoons vegetable oil, divided
¼ pound green onions, cut into 2-inch
   lengths, separating whites from tops
1 large red bell pepper, cut into strips
   Hot cooked vermicelli or thin spaghetti

Separate and rinse napa; pat dry. Thinly slice enough leaves crosswise to measure 8 cups; place in colander or large strainer. Pour boiling water over cabbage just until leaves wilt. Cool under cold water; drain thoroughly. Cut beef across grain into thin slices, then into strips. Combine 1 tablespoon stir-fry sauce and crushed red pepper in small bowl; stir in beef to coat. Heat 1 tablespoon oil in hot wok or large skillet over high heat. Add beef and stir-fry 1 minute; remove. Heat remaining 1 tablespoon oil in same pan; add white parts of green onions and stir-fry 1 minute. Add red bell pepper; stir-fry 2 minutes. Add green onion tops; stir-fry 2 minutes longer. Add beef, cabbage and remaining 5 tablespoons stir-fry sauce; cook and stir until vegetables are coated with sauce. Serve immediately over vermicelli.

Makes 4 servings

GLAZED PORK ROAST

1 (3-pound) boneless pork shoulder roast
   (Boston Butt)
1 cup Kikkoman Teriyaki Sauce
3 tablespoons brown sugar, packed
3 tablespoons dry sherry
1 teaspoon minced fresh ginger root
1 clove garlic, minced
¼ cup water
2 tablespoons sugar
1 tablespoon cornstarch

MICROWAVE DIRECTIONS: Pierce meaty parts of roast with fork; place in large plastic bag. Combine teriyaki sauce, brown sugar, sherry, ginger and garlic; pour over roast. Press air out of bag; tie top securely. Refrigerate 8 hours or overnight, turning bag over occasionally. Reserving marinade, remove roast and place, fat side down, in 8×8-inch shallow microwave-safe dish. Brush thoroughly with reserved marinade. Cover roast loosely with waxed paper. Microwave on Medium-high (70%) 30 minutes, or until meat thermometer inserted into thickest part registers 165°F., rotating dish once and brushing with marinade. Remove roast; let stand 10 minutes before slicing. Meanwhile, combine reserved marinade, water, sugar and cornstarch in 2-cup microwave-safe measuring cup. Microwave on High 3 minutes, until mixture boils and thickens, stirring occasionally. Serve teriyaki glaze with roast.

Makes 6 servings

GINGER BEEF WITH BOK CHOY

¾ pound boneless tender beef steak
   (sirloin, rib eye or top loin)
3 tablespoons Kikkoman Lite Soy Sauce,
   divided
1 tablespoon cornstarch
1 tablespoon dry sherry
1 teaspoon minced fresh ginger root
1 clove garlic, minced
¾ cup water
2 teaspoons cornstarch
½ pound bok choy cabbage or romaine
   lettuce
2 tablespoons vegetable oil, divided
1 medium onion, cut into ½-inch strips
1 tablespoon slivered fresh ginger root

Cut beef across grain into thin slices. Combine 1 tablespoon *each* lite soy sauce, cornstarch and sherry with minced ginger and garlic in medium bowl; stir in beef. Let stand 30 minutes. Meanwhile, combine water, 2 teaspoons cornstarch and remaining 2 tablespoons lite soy sauce; set aside. Separate and rinse bok choy; pat dry. Cut leaves crosswise into 1-inch strips, separating stems from leaves. Heat 1 tablespoon oil in hot wok or large skillet over high heat. Add beef and stir-fry 1 minute; remove. Heat remaining 1 tablespoon oil in same pan. Add onion and slivered ginger; stir-fry 2 minutes. Add bok choy stems; stir-fry 1 minute. Add leaves; stir-fry 1 minute longer. Add beef and soy sauce mixture; cook and stir until sauce boils and thickens. Serve immediately. *Makes 4 servings*

Ginger Beef with Bok Choy

Chinese Tea-Smoked Ribs

CHINESE TEA–SMOKED RIBS

16 bags or 6 tablespoons loose black tea
    leaves
1½ teaspoons fennel seed, crushed
  ½ teaspoon ground ginger
  ½ teaspoon ground cloves
  ½ teaspoon black pepper
    Nonstick cooking spray
  3 pounds pork spareribs, sawed into
    thirds across bones
  ½ cup Kikkoman Teriyaki Baste & Glaze
  1 tablespoon tomato catsup
  1 clove garlic, minced
  ⅛ teaspoon ground red pepper (cayenne)

Remove tea leaves from bags; combine with fennel, ginger, cloves and black pepper. Thoroughly spray large rack and large shallow baking pan with cooking spray. Sprinkle tea mixture evenly in pan. Cut ribs into 1-rib pieces and place, meaty side up, on rack over tea mixture. Cover pan with foil and bake at 350°F. 30 minutes. Meanwhile, combine teriyaki baste & glaze, catsup, garlic and red pepper; set aside. Remove ribs from oven; *reduce oven temperature to 325°F.* Reserving about 2 tablespoonfuls, brush both sides of ribs with baste & glaze mixture; return to oven and bake, uncovered, 40 minutes. Brush tops of ribs with reserved baste & glaze mixture; bake 5 minutes longer. Garnish as desired. *Makes 3 to 4 servings*

Beef with Leafy Greens

BEEF WITH LEAFY GREENS

¾ pound romaine lettuce
½ pound boneless tender beef steak
    (sirloin, rib eye or top loin)
4 tablespoons Kikkoman Stir-Fry Sauce,
    divided
1 clove garlic, minced
2 tablespoons vegetable oil, divided
1 medium onion, chunked
1 teaspoon minced fresh ginger root
8 cherry tomatoes, halved *or* 1 medium
    tomato, chunked
2 tablespoons chopped unsalted peanuts

Separate and rinse lettuce; pat dry. Cut leaves crosswise into 1-inch strips; set aside. Cut beef across grain into thin slices. Combine 1 tablespoon stir-fry sauce and garlic in small bowl; stir in beef to coat. Heat 1 tablespoon oil in hot wok or large skillet over high heat. Add beef and stir-fry 1 minute; remove. Heat remaining 1 tablespoon oil in same pan. Add onion and ginger; stir-fry 2 minutes. Add lettuce; stir-fry 2 minutes longer. Add beef, tomatoes and remaining 3 tablespoons stir-fry sauce; cook and stir until vegetables are coated with sauce and tomatoes are just heated through. Serve immediately with peanuts.

Makes 2 to 3 servings

PORK & VEGETABLES OVER CRUSTY NOODLE CAKE

½ pound boneless lean pork
3 tablespoons cornstarch, divided
4 tablespoons Kikkoman Soy Sauce,
    divided
1 clove garlic, minced
1 can (14 oz.) chicken broth
    Crusty Noodle Cake (recipe follows)
2 tablespoons vegetable oil, divided
1 teaspoon minced fresh ginger root
2 stalks celery, cut diagonally into thin
    slices
2 large carrots, cut into julienne strips
1 onion, thinly sliced
½ pound fresh bean sprouts

Cut pork across grain into thin slices, then into strips. Combine 1 tablespoon *each* cornstarch and soy sauce with garlic in small bowl. Stir in pork until coated; set aside. Combine remaining 2 tablespoons cornstarch, 3 tablespoons soy sauce and chicken broth; set aside. Prepare Crusty Noodle Cake. Heat 1 tablespoon oil in same skillet over high heat. Add pork and stir-fry 2 minutes; remove. Heat remaining 1 tablespoon oil in same skillet; add ginger and stir-fry 15 seconds. Add celery, carrots and onion; stir-fry 2 minutes. Add bean sprouts and stir-fry 2 minutes longer. Stir in pork and soy sauce mixture. Cook and stir until mixture boils and thickens, about 1 minute. Spoon over noodle cake and serve immediately.

Makes 4 to 6 servings

CRUSTY NOODLE CAKE

Cook *8 ounces vermicelli* according to package directions. Drain; rinse under cold water and drain thoroughly. Heat *1 tablespoon vegetable oil* in large, nonstick skillet over medium-high heat. Add vermicelli all at once; slightly spread to fill bottom of skillet to form noodle cake. Without stirring, cook 6 minutes, or until golden on bottom. Lift cake with wide spatula; add *1 tablespoon oil* to skillet. Turn cake over. Cook 6 minutes longer, or until golden brown, shaking skillet occasionally to brown evenly; remove to serving platter and keep warm.

POULTRY

SPICY CHICKEN

¾ pound boneless chicken
3 tablespoons Kikkoman Soy Sauce,
  divided
1 tablespoon cornstarch
1 tablespoon dry sherry
4 teaspoons water
2 tablespoons vegetable oil
1 teaspoon minced fresh ginger root
¾ teaspoon crushed red pepper
1 small onion, chunked
1 small red or green bell pepper, cut into
  matchsticks
1 small zucchini, cut into matchsticks
½ cup water

Cut chicken into thin slices. Combine chicken and 1 tablespoon soy sauce in small bowl; let stand 30 minutes. Meanwhile, combine remaining 2 tablespoons soy sauce, cornstarch, sherry and 4 teaspoons water. Heat oil in hot wok or large skillet over high heat. Add ginger and crushed red pepper; cook until fragrant. Add chicken and stir-fry 3 minutes. Add onion, bell pepper, zucchini and ½ cup water; mix well. Cover and cook 1 minute, or until vegetables are tender-crisp. Add soy sauce mixture; cook and stir until sauce boils and thickens.

Makes 4 servings

CHICKEN ADOBO

3 pounds frying chicken pieces
½ cup Kikkoman Soy Sauce
½ cup distilled white vinegar
2 tablespoons sugar
1 teaspoon pepper
6 large cloves garlic, pressed

MICROWAVE DIRECTIONS: Rinse chicken pieces and pat dry with paper towels. Combine soy sauce, vinegar, sugar, pepper and garlic in large microwave-safe casserole with lid; add chicken pieces, skin side down. Cover and microwave on High 10 minutes. Turn chicken pieces over; rearrange in dish. Cover and microwave on High 13 minutes longer, or until chicken is tender, rearranging pieces once. Serve immediately. *Makes 4 servings*

44

Spicy Chicken

Chinese-Style Pot Roast Chicken

CHINESE–STYLE POT ROAST CHICKEN

3 pounds frying chicken pieces
¼ cup Kikkoman Soy Sauce
2 tablespoons vegetable oil
1 tablespoon dry sherry
1 clove garlic, minced
2 stalks celery, cut diagonally into ¼-inch
    slices
2 green onions and tops, cut into 1-inch
    lengths
¾ cup water
1 tablespoon cornstarch
2 tablespoons Kikkoman Soy Sauce
1 teaspoon sugar

Rinse chicken pieces and pat dry with paper towels. Rub chicken thoroughly with ¼ cup soy sauce; let stand 15 minutes. Heat oil in Dutch oven or large skillet over medium heat; add chicken and brown slowly in hot oil. Add sherry and garlic; cover and simmer 30 minutes, or until tender. Remove chicken from pan; keep warm. Add celery and green onions to pan; cook 1 to 2 minutes. Combine water, cornstarch, 2 tablespoons soy sauce and sugar; stir into pan and cook until thickened. Serve sauce and vegetables over chicken. *Makes 4 servings*

SPICY SMOKED DUCK

1 (4- to 5-pound) frozen duckling, thawed
¼ cup Kikkoman Lite Soy Sauce
1 teaspoon liquid smoke seasoning
½ teaspoon fennel seed, well crushed
¼ teaspoon pepper
⅛ teaspoon ground cloves

Remove and discard giblets and neck from duckling cavity. Wash duckling; drain and gently pat dry with paper towels. Combine lite soy sauce, liquid smoke, fennel, pepper and cloves. Brush body cavity with sauce mixture. Place duckling, breast side up, on rack in roasting pan. Roast at 425°F. 1 hour. *Reduce oven temperature to 350°F.* Continue roasting 45 minutes, or until tender. Brush skin of duckling several times with sauce mixture during last 30 minutes of cooking time. Let stand 15 minutes before carving.   *Makes 4 servings*

LOTUS CHICKEN CHOP SUEY

½ chicken breast, skinned and boned
4 tablespoons Kikkoman Teriyaki Sauce,
     divided
1 cup water
2 tablespoons cornstarch
1 tablespoon dry sherry
1 large carrot, cut diagonally into ⅛-inch
     slices
1 onion, chunked and separated
⅛ teaspoon salt
¼ pound fresh bean sprouts
1 package (6 oz.) frozen Chinese pea
     pods, thawed and drained

MICROWAVE DIRECTIONS: Cut chicken into narrow strips; place in small bowl. Stir in 2 tablespoons teriyaki sauce; let stand 20 minutes. Meanwhile, blend water, cornstarch, sherry and remaining 2 tablespoons teriyaki sauce in 2-cup microwave-safe measuring cup. Microwave on High 4 minutes, until mixture boils and thickens, stirring occasionally to prevent lumping; set aside. Combine carrot, onion and salt in 2-quart microwave-safe casserole. Microwave, covered, on High 4 minutes, stirring after 2 minutes. Stir in bean sprouts; cover and microwave on High 1 minute. Stir in chicken; microwave, covered, on High 3 minutes, stirring once. Combine cornstarch mixture with chicken and vegetables. Microwave, uncovered, on High 1 minute. Stir in pea pods. Microwave, uncovered, on High 2 minutes, or until mixture is heated through, stirring once.   *Makes 2 to 3 servings*

ORANGE–CASHEW CHICKEN

1 pound boneless chicken breasts
½ cup Kikkoman Teriyaki Baste & Glaze
2 tablespoons orange juice
2 tablespoons dry white wine
2 tablespoons vegetable oil
1 green pepper, cut into thin strips
½ cup diagonally sliced celery
1 can (11 oz.) mandarin orange segments,
     drained
½ cup roasted cashews

Cut chicken into thin slices. Combine teriyaki baste & glaze, orange juice and wine; set aside. Heat oil in hot wok or large skillet over medium heat. Add chicken, green pepper and celery; stir-fry 3 to 4 minutes. Pour in baste & glaze mixture; cook and stir until chicken and vegetables are coated with sauce. Remove from heat; stir in orange segments and cashews. Serve immediately.   *Makes 4 servings*

MONGOLIAN POT

2 whole chicken breasts, skinned and
  boned
4 tablespoons Kikkoman Soy Sauce,
  divided
2 teaspoons minced fresh ginger root
½ teaspoon sugar
2 cans (10¼ oz. each) condensed chicken
  broth
4 soup cans water
1 large clove garlic, minced
½ pound cabbage, cut into ¾-inch chunks
  (about 4 cups)
¾ pound fresh spinach, trimmed, washed
  and drained
3 green onions and tops, cut into 1-inch
  lengths and slivered
4 ounces vermicelli or thin spaghetti,
  cooked and drained
¼ pound fresh mushrooms, sliced

Cut chicken into thin strips. Combine 2 tablespoons soy sauce, ginger and sugar in medium dish; stir in chicken. Let stand 15 minutes. Meanwhile, combine chicken broth, water, remaining 2 tablespoons soy sauce and garlic in deep electric skillet or electric wok; bring to boil. Reduce heat; keep broth mixture hot. Arrange cabbage, spinach, green onions, vermicelli and mushrooms on platter. Using chopsticks or tongs, let individuals select and add chicken, vegetables and vermicelli to hot broth. Cook chicken until tender, vegetables to desired doneness and vermicelli until heated through. Serve in individual bowls with additional soy sauce, as desired. When all foods are cooked, serve broth as soup. *Makes 4 to 6 servings*

SZECHUAN DRAGON STIR-FRY

1 whole chicken breast, skinned and
  boned
1 tablespoon cornstarch
4 tablespoons Kikkoman Soy Sauce,
  divided
½ teaspoon sugar
1 clove garlic, minced
1 cup water
4 teaspoons cornstarch
¼ to ½ teaspoon crushed red pepper
2 tablespoons vegetable oil, divided
2 carrots, cut diagonally into thin slices
1 onion, chunked
2 small zucchini, cut in half lengthwise,
  then diagonally chunked
¼ cup unsalted peanuts
  Hot cooked rice

Cut chicken into thin, narrow strips. Combine 1 tablespoon *each* cornstarch and soy sauce with sugar and garlic in small bowl; stir in chicken and set aside. Blend water, 4 teaspoons cornstarch, remaining 3 tablespoons soy sauce and red pepper; set aside. Heat 1 tablespoon oil in hot wok or large skillet over high heat. Add chicken and stir-fry 2 minutes; remove. Heat remaining 1 tablespoon oil in same pan. Add carrots and onion; stir-fry 3 minutes. Add zucchini; stir-fry 2 minutes. Add chicken and soy sauce mixture. Cook and stir until sauce boils and thickens. Just before serving, stir in peanuts. Serve immediately with rice.

Makes 4 servings

JADE & RUBY STIR-FRY

1 whole chicken breast, skinned and
    boned
1 pound fresh broccoli
2 tablespoons vegetable oil
1 medium onion, chunked
2 tablespoons water
2 medium-size red bell peppers, chunked
½ pound fresh mushrooms, quartered
⅓ cup Kikkoman Stir-Fry Sauce
¼ teaspoon crushed red pepper

Cut chicken into 1-inch square pieces. Remove flowerets from broccoli; cut into bite-size pieces. Peel stalks; cut into thin slices. Heat oil in hot wok or large skillet over high heat. Add chicken; stir-fry 1 minute. Add broccoli and onion; stir-fry 1 minute. Add water; cover and cook 2 minutes, stirring once. Add bell peppers and mushrooms; stir-fry 2 minutes. Stir in stir-fry sauce and crushed red pepper. Cook and stir until chicken and vegetables are coated with sauce. Serve immediately. *Makes 4 servings*

COLORFUL DRAGON STIR-FRY

1 whole chicken breast, skinned and
    boned
1 pound fresh broccoli
5 tablespoons Kikkoman Stir-Fry Sauce,
    divided
3 tablespoons vegetable oil, divided
1 medium onion, cut into thin wedges
1 medium carrot, cut diagonally into thin
    slices
2 tablespoons water

Cut chicken into ½-inch strips. Remove flowerets from broccoli; set aside. Peel stalks; cut into thin slices. Coat chicken with 1 tablespoon stir-fry sauce. Heat 1 tablespoon oil in hot wok or large skillet over high heat. Add chicken and stir-fry 3 minutes; remove. Heat remaining 2 tablespoons oil in same pan. Add onion; stir-fry 1 minute. Add broccoli and carrot; stir-fry 2 minutes longer. Pour water into pan. Reduce heat and simmer, covered, 3 minutes; stir once. Add remaining 4 tablespoons stir-fry sauce and chicken. Cook and stir just until chicken and vegetables are coated. Serve immediately. *Makes 4 servings*

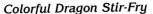

Colorful Dragon Stir-Fry

Dragon King's Tea-Smoked Chicken

DRAGON KING'S TEA–SMOKED CHICKEN

1 (3- to 3½-pound) whole frying chicken
⅓ cup Kikkoman Soy Sauce
2 tablespoons dry sherry
2 teaspoons minced fresh ginger root
¼ cup loose cinnamon-apple herb tea,
about 12 to 14 tea bags
2 tablespoons brown sugar, packed

Remove and discard giblets and neck from chicken. Rinse chicken under cold running water; drain well and pat dry with paper towels. Place chicken in large plastic food storage bag. Combine soy sauce, sherry and ginger; pour over chicken. Press air out of bag; close top securely. Turn over several times to coat cavity and outside of chicken. Refrigerate 8 hours or overnight, turning bag over occasionally. Combine herb tea with brown sugar; sprinkle to evenly cover bottom of foil-lined shallow baking pan. Place chicken, breast-side up, on rack over tea mixture. Cover pan with foil and bake in 350°F. oven 1 hour. Remove pan from oven; discard foil. *Increase oven temperature to 400°F.* Bake chicken 30 minutes longer, or until tender. Let stand 10 minutes before carving.
Makes 4 servings

SPICY CASHEW STIR–FRY

3 chicken breast halves, skinned and
boned
2 tablespoons vegetable oil
2 teaspoons minced fresh ginger root
6 to 8 whole red chili peppers
1 small onion, thinly sliced
1 small zucchini, thinly sliced
2 tablespoons chicken broth or water
1 tablespoon dry sherry
3 tablespoons Kikkoman Stir-Fry Sauce
½ cup unsalted roasted cashews

Cut chicken into thin slices. Place wok or large skillet over high heat until hot. Add oil, swirling to coat sides of pan. Add ginger and chili peppers; cook and stir until fragrant. Add chicken and stir-fry 3 minutes. Add onion, zucchini, broth, sherry and stir-fry sauce; cover and cook 1 minute, or until vegetables are tender-crisp. Stir in cashews; serve immediately.
Makes 4 servings

BEIJING CHICKEN

3 pounds frying chicken pieces
½ cup Kikkoman Teriyaki Sauce
1 tablespoon dry sherry
2 teaspoons minced fresh ginger root
½ teaspoon fennel seed, crushed
½ teaspoon grated orange peel
½ teaspoon honey

Rinse chicken pieces and pat dry with paper towels; place in large plastic bag. Combine teriyaki sauce, sherry, ginger, fennel, orange peel and honey; pour over chicken. Press air out of bag; tie top securely. Refrigerate 8 hours or overnight, turning bag over occasionally. Reserving marinade, remove chicken and place on rack of broiler pan. Broil 5 to 7 inches from heat source about 40 minutes, or until chicken is tender, turning pieces over and basting occasionally with reserved marinade.
Makes 4 servings

CHICKEN WITH BOK CHOY

½ chicken breast, skinned and boned
2 tablespoons cornstarch, divided
4 tablespoons Kikkoman Teriyaki Sauce,
    divided
1 tablespoon minced fresh ginger root
¾ cup water
1 pound bok choy cabbage or romaine
    lettuce
3 tablespoons vegetable oil, divided
1 onion, chunked and separated
½ pound fresh mushrooms, sliced
1 clove garlic, minced

Cut chicken into narrow strips. Combine 1 tablespoon *each* cornstarch and teriyaki sauce with ginger in small bowl; stir in chicken. Let stand 10 minutes. Meanwhile, combine water, the remaining 1 tablespoon cornstarch and 3 tablespoons teriyaki sauce; set aside. Separate and rinse bok choy; pat dry. Cut leaves crosswise into 2-inch strips, separating stems from leaves. Heat 1 tablespoon oil in hot wok or large skillet over high heat. Add chicken and stir-fry 1 minute; remove. Heat remaining 2 tablespoons oil in same pan. Add bok choy stems, onion, mushrooms and garlic; stir-fry 4 minutes. Add bok choy leaves; stir-fry 1 minute. Add chicken and teriyaki sauce mixture; cook and stir until sauce boils and thickens.   *Makes 2 to 3 servings*

KUNG PAO STIR-FRY

1 whole chicken breast, skinned and
    boned
2 tablespoons cornstarch, divided
3 tablespoons Kikkoman Teriyaki Sauce,
    divided
¼ teaspoon ground red pepper (cayenne)
¾ cup water
4 teaspoons distilled white vinegar
¾ pound romaine lettuce
2 tablespoons vegetable oil, divided
⅓ cup roasted peanuts

Cut chicken into thin strips. Combine 1 tablespoon *each* cornstarch and teriyaki sauce with red pepper in small bowl; stir in chicken. Let stand 15 minutes. Meanwhile, combine water, remaining 1 tablespoon cornstarch and 2 tablespoons teriyaki sauce with vinegar; set aside. Separate and rinse lettuce; pat dry. Cut leaves crosswise into 2-inch strips. Heat 1 tablespoon oil in hot wok or large skillet over high heat. Add chicken and stir-fry 2 minutes; remove. Heat remaining 1 tablespoon oil in same pan. Add lettuce; stir-fry 1 minute. Stir in chicken and teriyaki sauce mixture. Cook and stir until mixture boils and thickens. Remove from heat; stir in peanuts. Serve immediately.
Makes 4 servings

HOT CHICKEN WITH PEANUTS

½ pound boneless chicken breast
1 egg white
2 tablespoons Kikkoman Soy Sauce,
    divided
4 teaspoons cornstarch, divided
2 tablespoons dry sherry
1 teaspoon sugar
1 cup peanut oil
¼ teaspoon crushed red pepper
½ cup roasted peanuts
½ cup sliced green onions and tops

Cut chicken breast into ¾-inch cubes. Combine egg white, 1 tablespoon soy sauce and 3 teaspoons cornstarch in small bowl; stir in chicken. Cover and refrigerate 1 hour. Meanwhile, blend remaining 1 tablespoon soy sauce and 1 teaspoon cornstarch, sherry and sugar; set aside. Heat oil in wok or large skillet to 375°F. Stir chicken mixture; spoon into hot oil. Stir-fry 1 minute, or until chicken turns white; remove and drain on paper towels. Pour off all but 1 tablespoon oil from pan. Add red pepper and cooked chicken; stir-fry 1 minute. Add soy sauce mixture; cook and stir until chicken pieces are glazed with sauce. Stir in peanuts and green onions. Serve immediately.   *Makes 2 servings*

Firecracker Chicken Wings

FIRECRACKER CHICKEN WINGS

2 pounds chicken wings (about 10 wings)
1 tablespoon Kikkoman Stir-Fry Sauce
1 tablespoon dry sherry
⅔ cup water
⅓ cup Kikkoman Stir-Fry Sauce
2 teaspoons minced fresh ginger root
1 clove garlic, minced
⅛ teaspoon crushed red pepper
2 tablespoons vegetable oil
2 tablespoons chopped green onion and tops
2 tablespoons water
1½ teaspoons cornstarch
   Hot cooked rice

Disjoint chicken wings; discard tips (or save for stock). Combine 1 tablespoon stir-fry sauce and sherry in large bowl. Stir in chicken until well coated. Cover and refrigerate 30 minutes. Meanwhile, combine ⅔ cup water, ⅓ cup stir-fry sauce, ginger, garlic and red pepper; set aside. Heat oil in large skillet over medium heat. Add chicken and brown on all sides. Remove chicken; drain off oil. Pour stir-fry sauce mixture into same skillet. Add chicken; cover and simmer 5 minutes. Sprinkle green onion over chicken; cover and simmer 5 minutes longer, or until chicken is tender. Combine 2 tablespoons water and cornstarch; stir into skillet. Cook and stir until sauce boils and thickens. Serve chicken and sauce over rice. *Makes 4 servings*

GOLDEN CHICKEN STIR-FRY

1 whole chicken breast, skinned and
  boned
1 tablespoon cornstarch
5 tablespoons Kikkoman Teriyaki Sauce,
  divided
1 clove garlic, minced
1¼ cups regular-strength chicken broth
4 teaspoons cornstarch
  Boiling water
½ pound fresh bean sprouts
2 cups finely shredded lettuce
2 tablespoons vegetable oil, divided
2 medium carrots, cut into julienne strips
1 onion, chunked
2 teaspoons slivered fresh ginger root

Cut chicken into thin strips. Combine 1 tablespoon *each* cornstarch and teriyaki sauce with garlic in small bowl; stir in chicken. Let stand 15 minutes. Meanwhile, combine chicken broth, remaining 4 tablespoons teriyaki sauce and 4 teaspoons cornstarch; set aside. Pour boiling water over bean sprouts in bowl; let stand 1 minute. Drain; rinse under cold water and drain thoroughly. Toss sprouts with lettuce. Line serving platter with mixture; set aside. Heat 1 tablespoon oil in hot wok or large skillet over high heat. Add chicken and stir-fry 2 minutes; remove. Heat remaining 1 tablespoon oil in same pan. Add carrots, onion and ginger; stir-fry 4 minutes. Add chicken and teriyaki sauce mixture. Cook and stir until sauce boils and thickens. Turn out onto lined platter; toss to combine before serving. *Makes 4 servings*

LETTUCE-WRAPPED PLUM CHICKEN

  Orange-Plum Sauce (recipe follows)
1 whole chicken breast, skinned and
  boned
3 tablespoons Kikkoman Soy Sauce,
  divided
4 teaspoons cornstarch, divided
¼ cup water
2 tablespoons vegetable oil, divided
½ cup diced carrots
1 cup diced celery
½ cup diced onion
1 tablespoon minced fresh ginger root
8 large iceberg lettuce leaves

Prepare Orange-Plum Sauce; cool to room temperature. Meanwhile, dice chicken breast. Combine 1 tablespoon soy sauce and 3 teaspoons cornstarch in small bowl; stir in chicken. Let stand 10 minutes. Combine the remaining 2 tablespoons soy sauce, 1 teaspoon cornstarch and water; set aside. Heat 1 tablespoon oil in hot wok or large skillet over high heat. Add chicken and stir-fry 2 minutes; remove. Heat remaining 1 tablespoon oil in same pan. Add carrots and stir-fry 1 minute. Add celery, onion and ginger; stir-fry 2 minutes longer. Stir in chicken and soy sauce mixture. Cook and stir until mixture boils and thickens. To serve, spread about 2 teaspoons Orange-Plum Sauce in center of each lettuce leaf. Fill each leaf with about ¼ cup chicken mixture; fold lettuce around filling to enclose. *Makes 8 servings*

ORANGE-PLUM SAUCE

Blend *½ cup plum jam, ½ teaspoon grated fresh orange peel, 1 pressed garlic clove, 2 tablespoons Kikkoman Teriyaki Sauce, 2 tablespoons orange juice* and *1 teaspoon cornstarch* in small saucepan. Bring to boil over medium-high heat; reduce heat and simmer 1 minute, stirring constantly.

Golden Chicken Stir-Fry

Chicken Teriyaki Kabobs

CHICKEN TERIYAKI KABOBS

1½ pounds chicken breasts, skinned and
    boned
  1 bunch green onions, cut into 1-inch
    lengths
½ cup Kikkoman Soy Sauce
  2 tablespoons sugar
  1 teaspoon vegetable oil
  1 teaspoon minced fresh ginger root
  1 clove garlic, minced

Cut chicken into 1½-inch square pieces. Thread each of eight 6-inch bamboo or metal skewers alternately with chicken and green onion pieces. (Spear green onion pieces through side.) Place skewers in shallow pan. Combine soy sauce, sugar, oil, ginger and garlic; pour over skewers and brush chicken thoroughly with sauce. Marinate 30 minutes. Reserving marinade, remove skewers and place on rack of broiler pan. Broil 3 minutes; turn over and brush with reserved marinade. Broil 3 minutes longer, or until chicken is tender. *Makes 4 servings*

BRAISED CHINESE DUCKLING

1 (4- to 5-pound) frozen duckling, thawed
   and quartered
3 tablespoons Kikkoman Lite Soy Sauce,
   divided
1 tablespoon vegetable oil
2 tablespoons dry sherry
1 clove garlic, minced
1 teaspoon ginger juice*
4 green onions and tops, cut into 2-inch
   lengths
⅓ cup water
2 teaspoons cornstarch

Wash duckling quarters; dry with paper towels. Rub thoroughly with 2 tablespoons lite soy sauce. Let stand 30 minutes. Heat oil in Dutch oven or large skillet over medium heat. Brown duckling slowly in hot oil; drain off fat. Add sherry and garlic. Cover and cook over low heat 45 minutes, or until tender, turning quarters over once. Remove from pan; keep warm. Spoon off and discard excess fat from pan juices; return ⅓ cup juices to pan. Add remaining 1 tablespoon lite soy sauce, ginger juice and green onions; cook 1 minute. Combine water with cornstarch; stir into pan. Cook and stir until sauce boils and thickens. To serve, spoon sauce over duckling quarters. *Makes 4 servings*

*Peel fresh ginger root, then squeeze through garlic press.

SHANTUNG CHICKEN

1 whole chicken breast, skinned and
   boned
2 tablespoons cornstarch, divided
3 tablespoons Kikkoman Soy Sauce,
   divided
1 tablespoon dry sherry
1 clove garlic, minced
1 cup water
3 tablespoons vegetable oil, divided
½ pound fresh bean sprouts
¼ pound green onions and tops, cut into
   1½-inch lengths, separating whites
   from tops
1 tablespoon slivered fresh ginger root
1 tablespoon sesame seed, toasted
   Hot cooked noodles

Cut chicken into narrow strips. Combine 1 tablespoon *each* cornstarch and soy sauce with sherry and garlic in small bowl; stir in chicken. Let stand 5 minutes. Meanwhile, blend water, remaining 1 tablespoon cornstarch and 2 tablespoons soy sauce; set aside. Heat 1 tablespoon oil in hot wok or large skillet over high heat. Add chicken and stir-fry 2 minutes; remove. Heat remaining 2 tablespoons oil in same pan; add bean sprouts, white parts of green onions and ginger; stir-fry 3 minutes. Stir in chicken, soy sauce mixture, green onion tops and sesame seed. Cook and stir until mixture boils and thickens. Serve immediately over noodles. *Makes 4 servings*

MANDARIN CHICKEN SALAD

1 whole chicken breast, split
2 cups water
4 tablespoons Kikkoman Soy Sauce, divided
  Boiling water
¾ pound fresh bean sprouts
1 carrot, peeled and shredded
½ cup slivered green onions and tops
2 tablespoons minced fresh cilantro or parsley
¼ cup distilled white vinegar
2 teaspoons sugar
½ cup blanched slivered almonds, toasted

Simmer chicken in mixture of 2 cups water and 1 tablespoon soy sauce in covered saucepan 15 minutes, or until chicken is tender. Meanwhile, pour boiling water over bean sprouts. Drain; cool under cold water and drain thoroughly. Remove chicken and cool. (Refrigerate stock for another use, if desired.) Skin and bone chicken; shred meat with fingers into large mixing bowl. Add bean sprouts, carrot, green onions and cilantro. Blend vinegar, sugar and remaining 3 tablespoons soy sauce, stirring until sugar dissolves. Pour over chicken and vegetables; toss to coat all ingredients. Cover and refrigerate 1 hour. Just before serving, add almonds and toss to combine. *Makes 4 servings*

HEARTY CHICKEN STIR-FRY WITH NOODLES

1 whole chicken breast, skinned and boned
1 tablespoon cornstarch
5 tablespoons Kikkoman Teriyaki Sauce, divided
1 clove garlic, minced
1 cup water
4 teaspoons cornstarch
2 teaspoons tomato catsup
2 medium zucchini
2 cups uncooked fine egg noodles
2 tablespoons vegetable oil, divided
1 medium onion, chunked
10 cherry tomatoes, halved

Cut chicken into ½-inch square pieces. Combine 1 tablespoon *each* cornstarch and teriyaki sauce with garlic in small bowl; stir in chicken. Let stand 30 minutes. Meanwhile, combine water, remaining 4 tablespoons teriyaki sauce, 4 teaspoons cornstarch and catsup; set aside. Cut zucchini in half lengthwise, then diagonally into 1-inch pieces. Cook noodles according to package directions; drain and keep warm on serving plate. Heat 1 tablespoon oil in hot wok or large skillet over high heat. Add chicken and stir-fry 2 minutes; remove. Heat remaining 1 tablespoon oil in same pan. Add zucchini and onion; stir-fry 4 minutes. Add chicken, teriyaki sauce mixture and tomatoes. Cook and stir until sauce boils and thickens. Pour over noodles; toss to combine before serving. *Makes 4 servings*

Easy Chinese Roast Duck

EASY CHINESE ROAST DUCK

1 (4- to 5-pound) frozen duckling, thawed
    and quartered
1 tablespoon five-spice powder*
3 tablespoons Kikkoman Soy Sauce
1 tablespoon dry sherry
½ to ¾ teaspoon coarse-ground black
    pepper
    Hot cooked rice

Rinse duckling quarters; drain and dry thoroughly with paper towels. Discard excess fat. Pierce skin thoroughly with fork. Combine five-spice powder, soy sauce, sherry and pepper in large bowl. Add duckling quarters; rub with mixture and let stand 30 minutes. Place, skin-side up, on rack in shallow roasting pan. Bake in 350°F. oven 1 hour and 10 minutes. Remove from oven; drain off pan drippings. Turn oven temperature to broil and position oven rack 4 to 5 inches from heat source. Broil quarters 2 to 3 minutes, or until skin is crisp. Serve with rice.

Makes 4 servings

If not available, combine 1 teaspoon fennel seed, crushed, ½ teaspoon anise seed, crushed, and ½ teaspoon **each ground cinnamon, cloves and ginger.*

SEAFOOD

CRYSTAL SHRIMP WITH SWEET & SOUR SAUCE

½ cup Kikkoman Sweet & Sour Sauce
1 tablespoon water
2 teaspoons cornstarch
½ pound medium-size raw shrimp, peeled and deveined
1 egg white, beaten
2 tablespoons vegetable oil, divided
1 clove garlic, minced
2 carrots, cut diagonally into thin slices
1 medium-size green bell pepper, chunked
1 medium onion, chunked
1 tablespoon sesame seed, toasted

Blend sweet & sour sauce and water; set aside. Measure cornstarch into large plastic food storage bag. Coat shrimp with egg white; drain off excess egg. Add shrimp to cornstarch in bag; shake bag to coat shrimp. Heat 1 tablespoon oil in hot wok or large skillet over medium-high heat. Add garlic; stir-fry 10 seconds, or until fragrant. Add shrimp and stir-fry 2 minutes, or until pink; remove. Heat remaining 1 tablespoon oil in same pan over high heat. Add carrots, green pepper and onion; stir-fry 4 minutes. Add shrimp and sweet & sour sauce mixture. Cook and stir until shrimp and vegetables are coated with sauce. Remove from heat; stir in sesame seed. Serve immediately.

Makes 4 servings

ORIENTAL STEAMED FISH

4 white fish steaks, about ¾ inch thick
1 tablespoon slivered fresh ginger root
¼ cup orange juice
2 tablespoons Kikkoman Soy Sauce
1½ teaspoons distilled white vinegar
½ teaspoon brown sugar
1 teaspoon Oriental sesame oil
2 green onions and tops, minced

Place fish, in single layer, on oiled rack of bamboo steamer; sprinkle ginger evenly over fish. Set rack in large pot or wok of boiling water. (Do not allow water level to reach fish.) Cover and steam 8 to 10 minutes, or until fish flakes easily when tested with fork. Meanwhile, combine orange juice, soy sauce, vinegar and brown sugar in small saucepan; bring to boil. Remove from heat; stir in sesame oil. Arrange fish on serving platter; sprinkle green onions over fish and pour sauce over all. *Makes 4 servings*

海鮮食譜

Crystal Shrimp with Sweet & Sour Sauce

CHINESE PORCUPINE MEATBALLS

½ cup uncooked rice
6 ounces medium-size raw shrimp
1 pound ground pork
⅔ cup chopped green onions and tops
3 tablespoons Kikkoman Soy Sauce
1 tablespoon dry sherry
2 cloves garlic, pressed
Mandarin Peach Sauce (see page 37)

Cover rice with warm water and let stand 20 minutes; drain. Meanwhile, peel, devein and mince shrimp. Combine shrimp with pork, green onions, soy sauce, sherry, garlic and rice; mix well. Divide into 8 equal portions; shape portions into meatballs. Arrange meatballs on steamer rack. Set rack in large saucepan or wok of boiling water. (Do not allow water level to reach meatballs.) Cover and steam 45 minutes, or until meatballs are cooked. Serve with warm Mandarin Peach Sauce.

Makes 4 servings

Chinese Porcupine Meatballs

SEAFOOD AND VEGETABLE TEMPURA

1 pound large raw shrimp or prawns
½ pound raw sea scallops
½ pound fresh or thawed white fish fillets,
    about ½ inch thick
1 large green bell pepper, cut in
    1½×2-inch pieces
1 sweet potato, peeled and cut diagonally
    into ¼-inch-thick slices
1 large zucchini, cut into ¼-inch-thick
    slices
½ pound fresh green beans or asparagus
    tips, cut into bite-size pieces
Vegetable oil for frying
Tempura Batter (recipe follows)
Tempura Dipping Sauce (recipe follows)
    or Kikkoman Tempura Sauce

Peel shrimp, leaving tails on; devein. Score shrimp, opposite deveined side, being careful not to cut all the way through; lightly tap across shrimp with back of knife to open slightly. Cut scallops in half, if large, and cut fish into 1½×2-inch pieces. Drain seafood and vegetables thoroughly on layers of paper towels; arrange on large platter. Pour oil at least 2 inches deep into electric skillet or deep, wide skillet over medium-high heat; heat to 375°F. Meanwhile, prepare Tempura Batter. To deep fry shrimp, hold one at a time by tail and dip into batter. Drain off excess batter slightly and slide shrimp gently into hot oil. Repeat with 3 or 4 more shrimp. Fry about 1 minute; turn over and fry 1 minute longer, or until lightly browned. Dip and fry other ingredients in the same manner. Drain tempura on wire rack placed over cake pan. Skim any batter from oil with wire strainer. Serve immediately with Tempura Dipping Sauce.

Makes 6 to 8 servings

TEMPURA BATTER

Beat *1 large egg* thoroughly with wire whisk or hand rotary beater (not electric). Blend in *1¼ cups ice-cold water.* Sprinkle *2 cups sifted cake flour* evenly over liquid all at once. With same whisk or beater, stir in flour quickly only until flour is moistened and large lumps disappear. Batter should be very lumpy. Do not stir batter after it is mixed.

TEMPURA DIPPING SAUCE

1 cup chicken broth
⅓ cup Kikkoman Soy Sauce
2 tablespoons dry white wine
2 teaspoons sugar
½ teaspoon grated fresh ginger root

Combine broth, soy sauce, wine, sugar and ginger in small saucepan; bring to boil. Serve with tempura. (Or, prepare Kikkoman Tempura Sauce according to bottle instructions.)

STEAMED SOLE & VEGETABLES

4 tablespoons Kikkoman Soy Sauce,
   divided
3 tablespoons dry white wine
1½ teaspoons minced fresh ginger root
1 teaspoon onion powder
½ teaspoon sugar
4 fresh sole fillets (about 4 ounces each)
1 large carrot, cut into julienne strips
1 medium zucchini, cut into julienne strips
3 tablespoons minced green onions and
   tops, divided

Combine 3 tablespoons soy sauce, wine, ginger, onion powder and sugar in shallow dish. Add fillets, turning over to coat both sides well. Let stand 10 minutes, turning over once. Meanwhile, toss carrot and zucchini together with remaining 1 tablespoon soy sauce; pour off excess sauce. Turn out vegetables onto 8-inch round heatproof plate. Remove fillets from marinade; spread out flat. Sprinkle 2 tablespoons green onions evenly over fillets. Starting at thin end, roll up fillets, jelly-roll fashion. Arrange, seam-side down, on vegetables. Place plate on large steamer rack set in large pot or wok of boiling water. (Do not allow water level to reach plate.) Cover and steam 12 minutes, or until fish flakes easily when tested with fork. Sprinkle remaining 1 tablespoon green onion evenly over fish. *Makes 4 servings*

SHANGHAI SHRIMP STIR-FRY

2 tablespoons cornstarch, divided
3 tablespoons Kikkoman Soy Sauce,
   divided
1 tablespoon minced fresh ginger root
½ teaspoon sugar
½ pound medium-size raw shrimp, peeled
   and deveined
1¼ cups water
¼ teaspoon fennel seed, crushed
⅛ teaspoon ground cloves
⅛ teaspoon pepper
1 pound fresh broccoli
3 tablespoons vegetable oil, divided
1 onion, chunked and separated

Combine 1 tablespoon *each* cornstarch and soy sauce with ginger and sugar in small bowl; stir in shrimp. Let stand 10 minutes. Meanwhile, combine water, remaining 1 tablespoon cornstarch and 2 tablespoons soy sauce, fennel, cloves and pepper; set aside. Remove flowerets from broccoli; cut into bite-size pieces. Peel stalks; cut into thin slices. Heat 1 tablespoon oil in hot wok or large skillet over high heat. Add shrimp and stir-fry 1 minute; remove. Heat remaining 2 tablespoons oil in same pan. Add broccoli; stir-fry 2 minutes. Add onion; stir-fry 3 minutes longer. Stir in shrimp and soy sauce mixture; cook and stir until sauce boils and thickens. *Makes 4 servings*

Steamed Sole & Vegetables

Drunken Shrimp

DRUNKEN SHRIMP

1 pound medium-size raw shrimp
2 tablespoons dry sherry
2½ teaspoons cornstarch, divided
1 teaspoon sugar, divided
3 tablespoons Kikkoman Lite Soy Sauce
2 tablespoons water
1 tablespoon distilled white vinegar
2 tablespoons vegetable oil
¼ cup chopped green onions and tops
1 teaspoon minced fresh ginger root
1 clove garlic, minced

Peel shrimp, leaving shells on tails; devein. Combine sherry, 2 teaspoons cornstarch and ½ teaspoon sugar in medium bowl; stir in shrimp until well coated. Cover and refrigerate 30 minutes. Meanwhile, combine lite soy sauce, water, vinegar and remaining ½ teaspoon *each* cornstarch and sugar; set aside. Heat oil in hot wok or large skillet over medium-high heat. Add green onions, ginger and garlic; stir-fry 30 seconds. Add shrimp; stir-fry 3 minutes, or until pink. Pour in lite soy sauce mixture; cook and stir until sauce boils and thickens. Garnish as desired.

Makes 4 servings

IMPERIAL SESAME FISH

2 teaspoons sesame seed, toasted
¼ cup Kikkoman Soy Sauce
2 teaspoons distilled white vinegar
2 teaspoons minced fresh ginger root
½ teaspoon sugar
½ cup water
1½ pounds fresh or thawed fish fillets, ½ to
    ¾ inch thick
2 teaspoons cornstarch
1 green onion and top, chopped

Measure sesame seed into blender container; cover and process about 10 seconds, or until finely ground. Add soy sauce, vinegar, ginger and sugar; cover and process about 15 seconds, scraping down sides once. Remove 3 tablespoons sauce mixture from blender container; combine with water in small saucepan and set aside. Generously brush both sides of fish with remaining sauce. Broil about 5 minutes, or until fish flakes easily when tested with fork. Meanwhile, blend cornstarch with mixture in saucepan. Bring to boil; cook and stir until sauce thickens. Stir in green onion. Just before serving, spoon sauce over cooked fish. Serve with assorted vegetables. *Makes 4 to 6 servings*

SHRIMP–IN–SHELL

1 pound medium-size raw shrimp,
    unpeeled
½ cup regular-strength chicken broth
2 tablespoons cornstarch
3 tablespoons Kikkoman Soy Sauce
2 teaspoons sugar
3 tablespoons vegetable oil
1 tablespoon minced fresh ginger root
1 large clove garlic, minced
1 red bell pepper, cut into thin strips
¼ pound fresh snow peas, trimmed

Thoroughly rinse shrimp; devein. Let drain on several layers of paper towels. Combine chicken broth, cornstarch, soy sauce and sugar; set aside. Heat oil in hot wok or large skillet over high heat. Add ginger and garlic; stir-fry 30 seconds. Add shrimp; stir-fry 1 to 2 minutes, or until pink. Remove shrimp with slotted spoon, leaving oil in pan. Add red pepper and snow peas to same pan; stir-fry 1 minute. Stir in shrimp and soy sauce mixture. Cook and stir until mixture boils and thickens, about 1 minute.

Makes 4 to 6 servings

GRILLED ORIENTAL FISH STEAKS

4 fish steaks (halibut, salmon or
    swordfish), about ¾ inch thick
¼ cup Kikkoman Lite Soy Sauce
3 tablespoons minced onion
1 tablespoon chopped fresh ginger root
1 tablespoon sesame seed, toasted
½ teaspoon sugar

Place fish in single layer in shallow baking pan. Measure lite soy sauce, onion, ginger, sesame seed and sugar into blender container; process on low speed 30 seconds, scraping sides down once. Pour sauce over fish; turn over to coat both sides. Marinate 30 minutes, turning fish over occasionally. Remove fish and broil or grill 4 inches from heat source or moderately hot coals 5 minutes on each side, or until fish flakes easily when tested with fork. Garnish as desired. *Makes 4 servings*

MANDARIN FISH STEW

1½ pounds firm white fish fillets (halibut,
    sea bass, swordfish or shark), ¾ inch
    thick
⅔ cup Kikkoman Sweet & Sour Sauce
¼ cup water
1 tablespoon brown sugar, packed
1 tablespoon Kikkoman Soy Sauce
2 tablespoons vegetable oil
2 large stalks celery, cut diagonally into
    thin slices
1 medium carrot, cut diagonally into thin
    slices
1 small onion, chunked
1 clove garlic, minced
1 teaspoon minced fresh ginger root
1 small zucchini, cut in half lengthwise,
    then into ¼-inch slices

Cut fish into 2-inch pieces. Combine sweet & sour sauce, water, brown sugar and soy sauce; set aside. Heat oil in large saucepan or skillet over high heat. Add celery, carrot, onion, garlic and ginger; stir-fry 1 minute. Add zucchini and stir-fry 1 minute longer; remove vegetables. Place fish pieces in single layer in same pan. Pour sweet & sour sauce mixture over fish; bring to boil. Reduce heat and simmer, covered, 4 minutes. Turn fish over. Simmer 4 minutes longer, or until fish flakes easily when tested with fork. Gently stir in vegetables and heat through. Serve immediately. *Makes 4 to 6 servings*

SHRIMP & VEGETABLE STIR-FRY

2 tablespoons cornstarch, divided
4 tablespoons Kikkoman Teriyaki Sauce,
    divided
1 tablespoon minced fresh ginger root
½ pound medium-size raw shrimp, peeled
    and deveined
¾ cup water
2 tablespoons vegetable oil, divided
2 stalks celery, cut diagonally into
    ¼-inch-thick slices
1 medium-size red bell pepper, cut into
    1-inch squares
¼ pound green onions and tops, cut into
    1-inch lengths, separating whites
    from tops

Combine 1 tablespoon *each* cornstarch and teriyaki sauce with ginger in small bowl; add shrimp and stir to coat evenly. Let stand 15 minutes. Meanwhile, combine water, remaining 1 tablespoon cornstarch and 3 tablespoons teriyaki sauce; set aside. Heat 1 tablespoon oil in hot wok or large skillet over high heat. Add shrimp and stir-fry 1 minute; remove. Heat remaining 1 tablespoon oil in same pan. Add celery, red pepper and white parts of green onions; stir-fry 2 minutes. Stir in shrimp, teriyaki sauce mixture and green onion tops. Cook and stir until mixture boils and thickens. Serve over rice, if desired.

Makes 4 servings

Mandarin Fish Stew

Saucy Shrimp over Chinese Noodle Cakes

SAUCY SHRIMP OVER CHINESE NOODLE CAKES

Chinese Noodle Cakes (recipe follows)
1¼ cups water
2 tablespoons cornstarch, divided
4 tablespoons Kikkoman Soy Sauce,
    divided
1 teaspoon tomato catsup
½ pound medium-size raw shrimp, peeled
    and deveined
2 tablespoons vegetable oil, divided
1 clove garlic, minced
½ teaspoon minced fresh ginger root
1 green pepper, chunked
1 medium onion, chunked
2 stalks celery, cut diagonally into thin
    slices
2 tomatoes, chunked

Prepare Chinese Noodle Cakes. Combine water, 1 tablespoon cornstarch and 3 tablespoons soy sauce with catsup; set aside. Blend remaining 1 tablespoon cornstarch and 1 tablespoon soy sauce in small bowl; stir in shrimp until coated. Heat 1 tablespoon oil in hot wok or large skillet over high heat. Add shrimp and stir-fry 1 minute; remove. Heat remaining 1 tablespoon oil in same pan. Add garlic and ginger; stir-fry until fragrant. Add green pepper, onion and celery; stir-fry 4 minutes. Stir in soy sauce mixture, shrimp and tomatoes. Cook and stir until sauce boils and thickens. Cut Chinese Noodle Cakes into squares and serve with shrimp mixture. *Makes 4 servings*

CHINESE NOODLE CAKES

Cook *8 ounces capellini (angel hair pasta)* according to package directions. Drain; rinse under cold water and drain thoroughly. Heat *1 tablespoon vegetable oil* in large, non-stick skillet over medium-high heat. Add half the capellini; slightly spread to fill bottom of skillet to form noodle cake. Without stirring, cook 5 minutes, or until golden on bottom. Lift cake with wide spatula; add *1 tablespoon oil* to skillet and turn cake over. Cook 5 minutes longer, or until golden brown, shaking skillet occasionally to brown evenly; remove to rack and keep warm in 200°F. oven. Repeat with remaining capellini.

EMPEROR'S SWEET & SOUR FISH

1½ pounds fresh or thawed fish fillets,
    ½ inch thick
1 can (6 oz.) unsweetened pineapple juice
¼ cup Kikkoman Soy Sauce
¼ cup water
¼ cup sugar
2 tablespoons cornstarch
3 tablespoons vinegar
2 tablespoons tomato catsup
    Dash ground red pepper (cayenne)
¼ cup minced green onions and tops

MICROWAVE DIRECTIONS: Place fish in single layer in large microwave-safe dish; set aside. Combine pineapple juice, soy sauce, water, sugar, cornstarch, vinegar, catsup and red pepper in 2-cup microwave-safe measuring cup. Microwave on High 5 minutes, or until mixture boils and thickens, stirring occasionally to prevent lumping. Remove ¼ cup sauce and pour over fillets, turning each piece over to coat both sides. Keep remaining sauce warm. Cover fish with waxed paper; microwave on High 8 minutes, or until fish flakes easily when tested with fork, turning dish once. Remove fillets to serving platter with slotted spoon. To serve, drizzle warm sauce over fillets and sprinkle green onions over sauce. Pass remaining sauce. *Makes 4 to 6 servings*

Teriyaki Trout

TERIYAKI TROUT

4 medium trout (about 2 pounds), dressed
½ cup Kikkoman Teriyaki Sauce
¼ teaspoon grated lemon peel
3 tablespoons lemon juice
4 teaspoons Kikkoman Teriyaki Sauce

Score both sides of trout with diagonal slashes ¼ inch deep and 1 inch apart; place in large shallow pan. Pour ½ cup teriyaki sauce over trout, turning over to coat both sides well. Cover and refrigerate 1 hour, turning over once. Meanwhile, combine lemon peel and juice and 4 teaspoons teriyaki sauce; set aside. Reserving marinade, remove trout and place on rack of broiler pan. Broil 3 inches from heat source, 5 minutes on each side, or until fish flakes easily when tested with fork; brush occasionally with reserved marinade. Serve with lemon-teriyaki sauce.

Makes 4 servings

SZECHUAN SQUID STIR-FRY

1 pound fresh or thawed medium squid
   Boiling water
2 tablespoons cornstarch, divided
4 tablespoons Kikkoman Teriyaki Sauce,
   divided
¾ cup water
⅛ to ¼ teaspoon crushed red pepper
2 tablespoons vegetable oil, divided
1 red bell pepper, cut into ¼-inch strips
¼ pound green onions and tops, cut into
   2-inch lengths, separating whites
   from tops
1 tablespoon minced fresh ginger root
1 clove garlic, minced
3 cups shredded iceberg lettuce

Clean, skin and wash squid.* Cut body sacs into ¼-inch rings; place in bowl with tentacles. Add enough boiling water to cover; let stand 3 minutes. Drain; cool under cold water and drain thoroughly. Spread on paper towels and blot dry. Combine 1 tablespoon *each* cornstarch and teriyaki sauce in medium bowl; stir in squid. Let stand 10 minutes. Meanwhile, combine water, remaining 1 tablespoon cornstarch, 3 tablespoons teriyaki sauce and crushed red pepper; set aside. Heat 1 tablespoon oil in hot wok or large skillet over medium-high heat. Add squid and stir-fry 2 minutes; remove. Heat remaining 1 tablespoon oil in same pan. Add red bell pepper, white parts of green onions, ginger and garlic; stir-fry 2 minutes. Stir in squid, lettuce, green onion tops and teriyaki sauce mixture. Cook and stir until mixture boils and thickens. Serve immediately. *Makes 4 servings*

*To clean squid, carefully pull heads from body sacs; discard viscera. Set aside heads with tentacles. Remove transparent quills from inside sacs; wash insides thoroughly to remove all matter. Pull off speckled outer skin covering sacs. Cut tentacles from heads; discard hard "beaks" and heads.

SHANGHAI SWEET & SOUR FISH

1 cup water
¼ cup brown sugar, packed
¼ cup orange juice
2½ tablespoons cornstarch
3 tablespoons Kikkoman Lite Soy Sauce
3 tablespoons vinegar
1 tablespoon tomato catsup
2 teaspoons minced fresh ginger root
1 large onion, chunked and separated
1 large green pepper, chunked
1 large carrot, sliced diagonally into very
   thin slices
1 pound firm fish fillets (swordfish,
   halibut, mahi-mahi, shark), ¾ inch
   thick

MICROWAVE DIRECTIONS: Combine water, brown sugar, orange juice, cornstarch, lite soy sauce, vinegar, catsup and ginger; set aside. Combine onion, green pepper and carrot in large microwave-safe casserole. Cover and microwave on High 4 minutes. Stir in soy sauce mixture; cover and microwave on High 4 minutes. Remove from oven and let stand, covered, about 5 minutes. Meanwhile, cut fish into 1-inch pieces and place in single layer in separate small microwave-safe casserole. Cover and microwave on Medium-high (70%) 4 to 5 minutes, or until fish flakes easily when tested with fork, rotating dish once. Remove fish and add to vegetable mixture, stirring gently to combine. Serve immediately. *Makes 4 servings*

SIDE DISHES

CANTONESE CHICKEN SALAD

3 chicken breast halves
2 cups water
5 tablespoons Kikkoman Soy Sauce,
    divided
4 cups shredded iceberg lettuce
1 medium carrot, peeled and shredded
½ cup finely chopped green onions and
    tops
⅓ cup distilled white vinegar
2 tablespoons sesame seed, toasted
2 teaspoons sugar
½ teaspoon ground ginger
2 tablespoons minced fresh cilantro or
    parsley

Simmer chicken in mixture of water and 1 tablespoon soy sauce in covered saucepan 15 minutes, or until chicken is tender. Remove chicken and cool. (Refrigerate stock for another use, if desired.) Skin and bone chicken; shred meat into large mixing bowl. Add lettuce, carrot and green onions. Combine vinegar, remaining 4 tablespoons soy sauce, sesame seed, sugar and ginger; stir until sugar dissolves. Pour over chicken and vegetables; toss to coat all ingredients. Cover and refrigerate 1 hour. Just before serving, add cilantro and toss to combine. Garnish as desired. *Makes 6 servings*

SHRIMP FRIED RICE

2 eggs
2 tablespoons water
2 tablespoons vegetable oil
3 green onions and tops, chopped
3 cups cold, cooked rice
¼ pound cooked baby shrimp, chopped
3 tablespoons Kikkoman Soy Sauce

Beat eggs with water just to blend; set aside. Heat oil in hot wok or large skillet over medium heat. Add green onions; stir-fry 30 seconds. Add eggs and scramble. Stir in rice and cook until heated, gently separating grains. Add shrimp and soy sauce; cook and stir until heated through. Serve immediately.

Makes 6 servings

74

Cantonese Chicken Salad

FIRECRACKER SALAD

1 tablespoon sesame seed, toasted
2 tablespoons distilled white vinegar
2 teaspoons sugar
1 teaspoon minced fresh ginger root
4 teaspoons Kikkoman Soy Sauce
1 cup julienne-stripped radishes
1 cup julienne-stripped cucumber
4 cups finely shredded iceberg lettuce
1½ teaspoons minced fresh cilantro or
    parsley

Measure sesame seed, vinegar, sugar, ginger and soy sauce into jar with screw-top lid; cover and shake well until sugar dissolves. Combine radishes, cucumber and 3 tablespoons dressing; cover and refrigerate 30 minutes, stirring occasionally. Toss lettuce with cilantro in large bowl. Pour radish mixture and remaining dressing over lettuce. Toss lightly to combine. *Makes 6 servings*

STEAMED CHINESE BUNS

½ pound fresh bean sprouts, chopped
¼ pound medium-size raw shrimp, peeled,
    deveined and chopped
2 green onions and tops, chopped
1 clove garlic, minced
2 tablespoons cornstarch
2 tablespoons Kikkoman Soy Sauce
½ teaspoon ground ginger
1 can (7.5 oz.) refrigerated biscuits

MICROWAVE DIRECTIONS: Combine bean sprouts, shrimp, green onions, garlic, cornstarch, soy sauce and ginger in 1½-quart microwave-safe square dish. Microwave on High 6 minutes, until vegetables are tender-crisp, stirring once. Divide biscuit dough into 10 pieces. Flatten each piece into 3½-inch round, flouring hands if dough is sticky. Place about 2 tablespoonfuls shrimp mixture in center of each round. Bring edges together to enclose filling, pinching edges to seal securely. Place half the filled buns on 6- to 7-inch microwave-safe plate. Set plate in 1½-quart microwave-safe dish. Add ¼ cup hot water to bottom of dish. Microwave on High 5 minutes, or until buns are cooked. Repeat with remaining buns. Serve hot. *Makes 10 buns*

Firecracker Salad

Oriental Tea Eggs

ORIENTAL TEA EGGS

8 tea bags or 3 tablespoons loose black
    tea leaves
3 cups water
½ cup Kikkoman Teriyaki Sauce
8 eggs, room temperature

Combine tea bags, water and teriyaki sauce in medium saucepan; add eggs. Bring to full boil over high heat. Remove from heat; cover tightly and let stand 10 minutes. Remove eggs; reserve liquid. Place eggs under cold running water until cool enough to handle. Gently tap each eggshell with back of metal spoon until eggs are covered with fine cracks *(do not peel eggs)*. Return eggs to reserved liquid. Bring to boil; reduce heat, cover and simmer 25 minutes. Drain off liquid and refrigerate eggs until chilled, about 1 hour. Peel carefully before serving. *Makes 8 eggs*

HOT ORIENTAL SALAD

1 small head napa (Chinese cabbage)
¾ pound fresh spinach
1 tablespoon vegetable oil
2 cloves garlic, minced
½ teaspoon ground ginger
2 stalks celery, cut into julienne strips
½ pound fresh mushrooms, sliced
2 tablespoons Kikkoman Soy Sauce

Separate and rinse napa; pat dry. Slice enough leaves crosswise into 1-inch pieces to measure 8 cups. Wash and drain spinach; tear into pieces. Heat oil in Dutch oven over medium-high heat; add garlic and ginger. Stir-fry until garlic is lightly browned. Add celery; stir-fry 2 minutes. Add cabbage and mushrooms; stir-fry 2 minutes. Add spinach; stir-fry 2 minutes longer. Stir in soy sauce and serve immediately. *Makes 6 to 8 servings*

SPROUT–CUCUMBER SALAD

Boiling water
1 pound fresh bean sprouts
1 medium cucumber, thinly sliced
¼ cup finely chopped green onions and tops
2 tablespoons distilled white vinegar
2 tablespoons Kikkoman Soy Sauce
2 tablespoons vegetable oil
1¼ teaspoons sugar
1 tablespoon sesame seed, toasted (optional)

Pour boiling water over bean sprouts in colander; rinse immediately with cold water. Drain thoroughly. Arrange cucumber slices around outer edge of serving plate; set aside. Toss green onions with sprouts. Measure vinegar, soy sauce, oil and sugar in jar with screw-top lid; cover and shake well. Toss sprout mixture with about ⅔ of the dressing until thoroughly coated. Drizzle remaining dressing over cucumbers. Spoon sprout mixture in center of serving plate; sprinkle sesame seed over all. Serve immediately. *Makes 8 servings*

NEW YEAR FRIED RICE

3 strips bacon, diced
¾ cup chopped green onions and tops
⅓ cup diced red bell pepper
¼ cup frozen green peas, thawed
1 egg, beaten
4 cups cold, cooked rice
2 tablespoons Kikkoman Soy Sauce

Cook bacon in wok or large skillet over medium heat until crisp. Add green onions, red pepper and peas; stir-fry 1 minute. Add egg and scramble. Stir in rice and cook until heated, gently separating grains. Add soy sauce; cook and stir until heated through. Serve immediately. *Makes 6 to 8 servings*

SZECHUAN PORK SALAD

½ pound boneless lean pork
4 tablespoons Kikkoman Teriyaki Sauce, divided
⅛ to ¼ teaspoon crushed red pepper
1 cup water
2 tablespoons cornstarch
1 tablespoon distilled white vinegar
2 tablespoons vegetable oil, divided
1 onion, chunked and separated
12 radishes, thinly sliced
2 medium zucchini, cut into julienne strips
Salt
4 cups shredded lettuce

Cut pork across grain into thin slices, then into narrow strips. Combine pork, 1 tablespoon teriyaki sauce and red pepper in small bowl; set aside. Combine water, cornstarch, remaining 3 tablespoons teriyaki sauce and vinegar; set aside. Heat 1 tablespoon oil in hot wok or large skillet over high heat. Add pork and stir-fry 2 minutes; remove. Heat remaining 1 tablespoon oil in same pan. Add onion; stir-fry 2 minutes. Add radishes and zucchini; sprinkle lightly with salt and stir-fry 1 minute longer. Stir in pork and teriyaki sauce mixture. Cook and stir until mixture boils and thickens. Spoon over bed of lettuce on serving platter; serve immediately. *Makes 2 to 3 servings*

BEAN SPROUT & SPINACH SALAD

    Boiling water
 1 pound fresh spinach, washed
 ½ pound fresh bean sprouts
 1 tablespoon sugar
 4 teaspoons distilled white vinegar
 1 tablespoon Kikkoman Soy Sauce
 1 teaspoon sesame seed, toasted

Pour boiling water over spinach in colander; rinse immediately with cold water. Drain thoroughly and place in medium serving bowl. Repeat procedure with bean sprouts and place in same bowl. Combine sugar, vinegar, soy sauce and sesame seed; pour over vegetables and toss to combine. Cover and refrigerate at least 1 hour before serving.   *Makes 4 servings*

LUCKY DAY STIR-FRY

 ⅓ cup Kikkoman Stir-Fry Sauce
 1 large clove garlic, pressed
 ½ pound fresh asparagus
 2 tablespoons vegetable oil
 1 medium onion, sliced
 ½ pound fresh snow peas, trimmed
 1 large red bell pepper, cut into ½-inch
    strips
10 to 12 ears canned whole baby corn,
    rinsed

Combine stir-fry sauce and garlic; set aside. Cut asparagus into 2-inch pieces. Heat oil in hot wok or large skillet over high heat. Add asparagus and onion; stir-fry 2 minutes. Add snow peas; stir-fry 2 minutes. Add red pepper; stir-fry 2 minutes. Add corn; stir-fry 1 minute. Pour in stir-fry sauce mixture; cook and stir until vegetables are coated with sauce. Serve immediately.

Makes 6 servings

Lucky Day Stir-Fry

"Crab" & Cucumber Noodle Salad

"CRAB" & CUCUMBER NOODLE SALAD

8 ounces uncooked vermicelli
3 green onions and tops
¼ pound imitation crabmeat, shredded
1 cucumber, halved, seeded and cut into
   julienne strips
2 tablespoons chopped fresh cilantro
2 tablespoons vegetable oil
2 tablespoons minced fresh ginger root
2 large cloves garlic, minced
3 tablespoons Kikkoman Lite Soy Sauce
3 tablespoons distilled white vinegar
2 teaspoons sugar
4 teaspoons Oriental or dark sesame oil

Cook vermicelli according to package directions, omitting salt; drain. Rinse with cold water; drain thoroughly. Separate white parts of green onions from tops; chop whites. Cut tops into thin strips. Combine vermicelli, crabmeat, cucumber, cilantro and green onion tops in large bowl. Heat oil in small skillet over medium heat. Add whites of green onions, ginger and garlic; stir-fry 1 minute. Remove pan from heat; stir in lite soy sauce, vinegar, sugar and sesame oil until sugar dissolves. Pour over vermicelli mixture and toss to combine. Cover and refrigerate 1 hour, tossing occasionally. *Makes 6 servings*

PAGODA FRIED RICE

2 strips bacon, cut crosswise into
   ¼-inch-wide pieces
6 green onions and tops, thinly sliced
1 egg, beaten
4 cups cold, cooked rice
2 tablespoons Kikkoman Soy Sauce

Cook bacon in hot wok or large skillet over medium heat until crisp. Add green onions and stir-fry 1 minute. Add egg and scramble. Stir in rice and cook until heated through, gently separating grains. Add soy sauce and stir until mixture is well blended. *Makes 6 servings*

ORIENTAL CHICKEN & CABBAGE SALAD

4 chicken breast halves, skinned and
   boned
2 tablespoons Kikkoman Lite Soy Sauce
2 teaspoons lemon juice
1 teaspoon minced fresh ginger root
1 clove garlic, minced
3 cups shredded cabbage
1 cup shredded carrots
¼ pound fresh bean sprouts
   Lemon-Soy Dressing (recipe follows)

Place chicken in large plastic food storage bag. Combine lite soy sauce, lemon juice, ginger and garlic; pour over chicken. Press air out of bag; close top securely. Turn over several times to coat pieces well. Refrigerate 45 minutes, turning bag over occasionally. Meanwhile, combine cabbage, carrots and bean sprouts in large bowl. Prepare Lemon-Soy Dressing. Pour over vegetables; toss well to combine. Cover and refrigerate; toss occasionally. Remove chicken from marinade and place on rack of broiler pan. Broil 5 minutes on each side, or until tender. Slice each breast crosswise into 4 pieces and serve with salad. *Makes 4 servings*

LEMON-SOY DRESSING

2 tablespoons vegetable oil
2 tablespoons lemon juice
1 tablespoon Kikkoman Lite Soy Sauce
1 tablespoon honey
½ teaspoon dry mustard
¼ teaspoon celery seed

Thoroughly combine vegetable oil, lemon juice, lite soy sauce, honey, mustard, and celery seed in jar with screwtop lid; cover and shake well.

SOY-SPINACH SALAD

1 pound fresh spinach, washed and
   drained
4 medium-size fresh mushrooms, sliced
2 tablespoons vinegar
2 tablespoons water
1 tablespoon Kikkoman Soy Sauce
1 tablespoon vegetable oil
1½ teaspoons sugar

Tear spinach into bite-size pieces; place in large salad bowl and top with mushrooms. Combine vinegar, water, soy sauce, oil and sugar in small saucepan; bring to boil. Pour hot dressing over vegetables and quickly toss until spinach wilts. Serve immediately. *Makes 4 servings*

82

Mu Shu Pork (page 101)

CHINESE COOKING

APPETIZERS

SHRIMP TOAST

12 large shrimp, shelled and deveined,
    leaving tails intact
 1 egg
2½ tablespoons cornstarch
 ¼ teaspoon salt
   Pinch pepper
 3 slices white sandwich bread, crusts
    removed and quartered
 1 hard-cooked egg yolk, cut into ½-inch
    pieces
 1 slice cooked ham, cut into ½-inch pieces
 1 green onion, finely chopped
   Vegetable oil for frying

1. Cut down back of shrimp; press gently to flatten. Beat the 1 egg, cornstarch, salt and pepper in large bowl until blended. Add shrimp to egg mixture; toss to coat well.

2. Place 1 shrimp cut-side down on each bread piece. Press shrimp gently into bread. Brush or rub small amount of egg mixture over each shrimp.

3. Place 1 piece each of egg yolk and ham and a scant ¼ teaspoon onion on top of each shrimp.

4. Heat oil in wok or large skillet over medium-high heat to 375°F. Cook 3 or 4 shrimp-bread pieces at a time until golden, 1 to 2 minutes on each side. Drain on paper towels.

Makes 1 dozen

GREEN ONION CURLS

 6 to 8 medium green onions
   Cold water
10 to 12 ice cubes

1. Trim bulbs (white part) from onions; reserve for another use. Trim remaining stems (green part) to 4-inch lengths.

2. Using sharp scissors, cut each section of green stems lengthwise into very thin strips down to beginning of stems. Cut 6 to 8 strips in each stem section.

3. Fill large bowl about half full with cold water. Add green onions and ice cubes. Refrigerate until onions curl, about 1 hour. Drain and use for garnish.

Makes 6 to 8 curls

Shrimp Toast

Wonton Soup

HAM AND CHICKEN ROLLS

2 whole boneless, skinless chicken
   breasts
½ teaspoon salt
¼ teaspoon pepper
¼ teaspoon Chinese five-spice powder
⅛ teaspoon garlic powder
4 slices cooked ham (about 1 ounce each)
1 egg, beaten
2 tablespoons milk
¼ cup all-purpose flour
4 spring roll or egg roll wrappers
   Vegetable oil for frying

1. Cut each chicken breast in half. Using a mallet or rolling pin, pound chicken breasts until very thin.

2. Combine salt, pepper, five-spice powder and garlic powder in small bowl. Sprinkle about ¼ teaspoon spice mixture over each flattened chicken breast.

3. Tightly roll up each ham slice and place on top of chicken; roll chicken around ham, tucking in ends.

4. Combine egg and milk in shallow dish. Coat each chicken piece lightly with flour, then dip into egg-milk mixture. Place each piece diagonally onto a spring roll wrapper. Roll up securely, folding in ends. Brush end corner with egg mixture and pinch to seal.

5. Heat oil in wok or large skillet over high heat to 375°F. Cook 3 or 4 rolls at a time until golden and chicken is cooked through, about 5 minutes. Drain on paper towels. Cool slightly. Cut into 1-inch diagonal slices to serve. *Makes 4 rolls*

WONTON SOUP

½ cup finely chopped cabbage
4 ounces shelled, deveined shrimp, finely
    chopped
8 ounces lean ground pork
3 green onions, finely chopped
1 egg, lightly beaten
1½ tablespoons cornstarch
2 teaspoons soy sauce
1 teaspoon oyster sauce
2 teaspoons sesame oil, divided
48 wonton wrappers (about 1 pound)
1 egg white, lightly beaten
¾ pound bok choy or napa cabbage
6 cups chicken broth
1 cup thinly sliced Barbecued Pork (see
    page 88)
3 green onions, thinly sliced

1. For filling, squeeze cabbage to remove as much moisture as possible. Place cabbage in large bowl. Add shrimp, pork, chopped onions, whole egg, cornstarch, soy sauce, oyster sauce and 1½ teaspoons of the sesame oil; mix well.

2. For wontons, work with about 12 wrappers at a time, keeping remaining wrappers covered with plastic wrap. Place 1 wonton wrapper on work surface with one point facing you. Mound 1 teaspoon filling in bottom corner. Fold bottom corner over filling.

3. Moisten side corners with egg white. Bring side corners together, overlapping slightly. Pinch together firmly to seal. Cover finished wontons with plastic wrap while you fill remaining wontons. (Cook immediately, refrigerate up to 8 hours or freeze in resealable plastic bag.)

4. Cut bok choy stems into 1-inch-thick slices; cut leaves in half crosswise.

5. Cook wontons in large pot of boiling water until filling is no longer pink, about 4 minutes (6 minutes if frozen). Drain, then place in bowl of cold water to prevent wontons from sticking together.

6. Bring chicken broth to a boil in large saucepan. Add bok choy and remaining ½ teaspoon sesame oil; cook 2 minutes. Drain wontons and add to hot broth. Add slices of Barbecued Pork and sliced onions. *Makes 6 servings*

BARBECUED PORK

¼ cup soy sauce
2 tablespoons dry red wine
1 tablespoon brown sugar
1 tablespoon honey
2 teaspoons red food coloring (optional)
½ teaspoon ground cinnamon
1 green onion, cut in half
1 clove garlic, crushed
2 whole pork tenderloins (about
    12 ounces each), trimmed
  Green Onion Curls (see page 84), for
    garnish

1. Combine soy sauce, wine, sugar, honey, food coloring, cinnamon, onion and garlic in large bowl. Add pork, turning tenderloins to coat completely. Cover and refrigerate 1 hour or overnight, turning meat occasionally.

2. Drain pork, reserving marinade. Place tenderloins on wire rack over a baking pan. Bake in preheated 350°F oven, turning and basting often with reserved marinade, until cooked through, about 45 minutes.

3. Remove pork from oven; cool. Cut into diagonal slices. Garnish with Green Onion Curls.   *Makes about 8 appetizer servings*

GOW GEES

1 ounce dried mushrooms
48 wonton wrappers (about 1 pound)
2 ounces shelled, deveined shrimp
4 ounces boneless lean pork
3 green onions
2 teaspoons soy sauce
½ teaspoon minced fresh ginger
1 clove garlic, crushed
  Vegetable oil for frying
  Sweet and Sour Sauce (recipe follows)

1. Place mushrooms in bowl and cover with hot water. Let stand 30 minutes; drain and squeeze out excess water. Cut off and discard stems.

2. Cut wonton wrappers into circles using 3-inch cookie cutter or clean can. Cover with plastic wrap.

3. Finely chop shrimp, pork, onions and mushrooms with cleaver or food processor; transfer to large bowl. Add soy sauce, ginger and garlic; mix well.

4. Place 1 level teaspoon pork mixture in center of each wonton circle. Brush edges with water. Fold circles in half over filling, pressing edges together to seal.

5. Heat oil in wok or large skillet over high heat to 375°F. Cook 8 to 10 gow gees at a time until golden, 2 to 3 minutes. Drain on paper towels. Serve with Sweet and Sour Sauce.

Makes 4 dozen

SWEET AND SOUR SAUCE

1 cup water
½ cup distilled white vinegar
½ cup sugar
¼ cup tomato paste
4 teaspoons cornstarch

Combine water, vinegar, sugar, tomato paste and cornstarch in small saucepan. Bring to a boil over medium heat, stirring constantly. Boil and stir 1 minute.

Barbecued Pork

Hors d'Oeuvre Rolls

HORS D'OEUVRE ROLLS

½ cup Chinese-style thin egg noodles,
    broken into 1-inch pieces
2 tablespoons butter or margarine
4 ounces boneless lean pork, finely
    chopped
6 medium fresh mushrooms, finely
    chopped
6 green onions, finely chopped
8 ounces shelled, deveined shrimp,
    cooked and finely chopped
1 hard-cooked egg, finely chopped
1½ tablespoons dry sherry
½ teaspoon salt
⅛ teaspoon pepper
2 sheets commercial puff pastry dough or
    40 wonton wrappers
1 egg, beaten
    Vegetable oil for frying
    Sweet and Sour Sauce (see page 88),
    optional

1. Cook noodles according to package directions until tender but still firm, 2 to 3 minutes. Drain and rinse under cold running water and drain again. Chop noodles finely.

2. Heat butter in wok or large skillet over medium-high heat. Add pork and stir-fry until browned, about 5 minutes. Add mushrooms and onions; stir-fry 2 minutes. Remove from heat and add shrimp, hard-cooked egg, cooked noodles, sherry, salt and pepper; mix well.

3. If using puff pastry, roll and trim each sheet into a 15×12-inch rectangle. Cut each rectangle into 20 (3-inch) squares.

4. Place 1 tablespoon pork mixture across center of each pastry square or wonton wrapper. Brush edges lightly with beaten egg. Roll up tightly around filling and pinch edges slightly to seal.

5. Heat oil in wok or large skillet to 375°F. Cook 6 to 8 rolls at a time until golden and crisp, 3 to 5 minutes. Drain on paper towels. Serve with Sweet and Sour Sauce, if desired.

Makes 40 rolls

CRAB COMBINATION SOUP

1 ounce dried mushrooms
3 tablespoons cornstarch
6 tablespoons water, divided
1½ tablespoons dry sherry
4 teaspoons soy sauce
1 teaspoon vegetable oil
1 egg, lightly beaten
6 cups chicken broth
6 ounces fresh or thawed frozen crab
    meat, flaked
4 ounces fresh or thawed frozen sea
    scallops, rinsed and thinly sliced
½ cup bamboo shoots (½ of 8-ounce can),
    drained and cut into matchstick
    pieces
8 green onions, chopped
½ teaspoon minced fresh ginger
2 egg whites

1. Place mushrooms in bowl and cover with hot water. Let stand 30 minutes. Drain and squeeze out excess water. Remove and discard stems; cut caps into thin slices.

2. Combine cornstarch, 4 tablespoons of the water, the sherry and soy sauce in small bowl; mix well and set aside.

3. Heat oil in small skillet over medium-high heat. Add egg and tilt pan to cover bottom. Cook just until egg is set. Loosen edges; turn omelet and cook other side. Remove omelet from pan, roll up and cut into thin strips.

4. Pour broth into 3-quart saucepan. Bring to a boil. Stir in mushrooms, sliced egg, crab meat, scallops, bamboo shoots, onions and ginger. Bring back to a boil.

5. Stir cornstarch mixture; pour into soup. Bring back to a boil. Beat egg whites and remaining 2 tablespoons water in small bowl. Stirring constantly, drizzle egg whites slowly into soup.

Makes 6 servings

LONG SOUP

1½ tablespoons vegetable oil
8 ounces boneless lean pork, cut into thin strips
4 to 6 ounces cabbage (¼ of small head), shredded
6 cups chicken broth
2 tablespoons soy sauce
½ teaspoon minced fresh ginger
4 ounces Chinese-style thin egg noodles
8 green onions, diagonally cut into ½-inch slices

1. Heat oil in wok or large skillet over medium-high heat. Add pork and cabbage; stir-fry until pork is cooked through and no longer pink, about 5 minutes.

2. Add chicken broth, soy sauce and ginger to wok. Bring to a boil; reduce heat and simmer 10 minutes.

3. Stir in noodles and onions. Cook just until noodles are tender, 1 to 4 minutes. *Makes about 4 servings*

STUFFED MUSHROOMS

24 fresh medium mushrooms (about 1 pound)
6 ounces boneless lean pork
¼ cup whole water chestnuts (¼ of 8-ounce can)
3 green onions
½ small red or green bell pepper
1 small stalk celery
1 teaspoon cornstarch
1 teaspoon minced fresh ginger
2 teaspoons dry sherry
1 teaspoon soy sauce
½ teaspoon hoisin sauce
1 egg white
Vegetable oil for frying
Batter (recipe follows)
½ cup all-purpose flour

1. Clean mushrooms by wiping with a damp paper towel. Remove stems; chop stems finely and transfer to large bowl.

2. Finely chop pork, water chestnuts, onions, red pepper and celery with cleaver or food processor. Add to chopped mushroom stems. Add cornstarch, ginger, sherry, soy sauce, hoisin sauce and egg white; mix well.

3. Spoon pork mixture into mushroom caps, mounding in center. Heat oil in wok or large skillet over high heat to 375°F.

4. Prepare Batter. Dip mushrooms in flour, then in batter, coating completely. Cook 6 to 8 mushrooms at a time until golden, about 5 minutes. Drain on paper towels. *Makes 2 dozen*

BATTER

½ cup cornstarch
½ cup all-purpose flour
1½ teaspoons baking powder
¾ teaspoon salt
⅓ cup milk
⅓ cup water

Combine cornstarch, flour, baking powder and salt in medium bowl. Stir in milk and water; blend well.

Long Soup

FRIED WONTONS

1 ounce dried mushrooms
1 pound boneless lean pork
4 ounces fresh spinach
1½ tablespoons dry sherry
4 teaspoons soy sauce, divided
¼ teaspoon pepper
48 wonton wrappers (about 1 pound)
1 can (6 ounces) pineapple juice
½ cup distilled white vinegar
1 tablespoon catsup
½ cup sugar
1½ tablespoons cornstarch
¼ cup water
½ cup Chinese Mixed Pickled Vegetables
    (see page 140)
    Vegetable oil for frying

1. Place mushrooms in bowl and cover with hot water. Let stand 30 minutes. Drain and squeeze out excess water. Cut off and discard stems.

2. Finely chop pork, spinach and mushrooms with cleaver or food processor; transfer to large bowl. Add sherry, 2 teaspoons of the soy sauce and the pepper; mix well.

3. For wontons, work with about 12 wrappers at a time keeping remaining wrappers covered with plastic wrap. Spoon 1 rounded teaspoon pork mixture onto center of each wonton wrapper. Gather edges around filling, pressing firmly at top to seal.

4. Combine pineapple juice, vinegar, catsup, sugar and remaining 2 teaspoons soy sauce in small saucepan. Bring to a boil. Blend cornstarch and water in small cup; stir into pineapple mixture. Reduce heat; cook and stir until thickened, about 3 minutes. Stir in Chinese Mixed Pickled Vegetables; keep warm.

5. Heat oil in wok or large skillet over medium-high heat to 375°F. Cook 8 to 10 wontons at a time until golden and crisp, 2 to 3 minutes. Drain on paper towels. To serve, pour pineapple mixture over wontons. *Makes 4 dozen*

CHICKEN AND BANANA SQUARES

2 whole boneless, skinless chicken
    breasts, cooked
2 ripe medium bananas
6 slices white sandwich bread, trimmed
    and quartered
4 eggs
½ cup milk
½ cup all-purpose flour
4 cups soft bread crumbs (10 to 12 bread
    slices)
    Vegetable oil for frying

1. Cut chicken breasts into 8 pieces, then cut each of those pieces into thirds, yielding 24 pieces total.

2. Cut each banana lengthwise into quarters. Cut each quarter into thirds, yielding 24 pieces total.

3. Beat eggs and milk in medium bowl until blended. Brush one side of the 24 bread pieces with egg mixture. Place 1 piece of chicken and 1 piece of banana on each egg-glazed bread piece.

4. Place flour in one bowl and soft bread crumbs in another. Coat each chicken-banana square lightly with flour, dip in egg mixture, then coat with bread crumbs. Dip in egg mixture again and coat with crumbs.

5. Heat oil in wok or large skillet over high heat to 375°F. Cook 4 to 6 squares at a time until golden, 2 to 3 minutes. Drain on paper towels. *Makes 2 dozen*

POT STICKERS

2 cups all-purpose flour
¾ cup plus 2 tablespoons boiling water
½ cup very finely chopped napa cabbage
8 ounces lean ground pork
2 tablespoons finely chopped water
    chestnuts
1 green onion, finely chopped
1½ teaspoons soy sauce
1½ teaspoons dry sherry
½ teaspoon minced fresh ginger
1½ teaspoons cornstarch
½ teaspoon sesame oil
¼ teaspoon sugar
2 tablespoons vegetable oil, divided
⅔ cup chicken broth, divided
    Soy sauce, vinegar and chili oil

1. Place flour in large bowl and make a well in center. Pour in boiling water; stir with wooden spoon until dough begins to hold together. Knead dough until smooth and satiny on lightly floured surface, about 5 minutes. Cover and let rest 30 minutes.

2. For filling, squeeze cabbage to remove as much moisture as possible; place in large bowl. Add pork, water chestnuts, onion, soy sauce, sherry, ginger, cornstarch, sesame oil and sugar; mix well.

3. Divide dough into 2 equal portions; cover 1 portion with plastic wrap or a clean towel while you work with the other portion. Roll out dough to ⅛-inch thickness on lightly floured work surface. Cut out 3-inch circles with round cookie cutter or clean can. Place 1 rounded teaspoon filling in center of each dough circle.

4. To shape each pot sticker, lightly moisten edges of dough circle with water; fold in half. Starting at one end, pinch curled edges together making 4 pleats along edge. Set dumpling down firmly seam-side up. Cover finished pot stickers while you make remaining dumplings. (Cook dumplings immediately, refrigerate for up to 4 hours or freeze in resealable plastic bag.)

5. To cook pot stickers, heat 1 tablespoon of the vegetable oil in large nonstick skillet over medium heat. Set ½ of pot stickers in pan seam side up. (If cooking frozen dumplings, do not thaw.) Cook until bottoms are golden brown, 5 to 6 minutes. Pour in ⅓ cup of the chicken broth. Cover tightly, reduce heat and cook until all liquid is absorbed, about 10 minutes (15 minutes if frozen). Repeat with remaining vegetable oil, pot stickers and chicken broth.

6. Place pot stickers browned side up on serving platter. Serve with soy sauce, vinegar and chili oil for dipping.

Makes 32 pot stickers

Pot Stickers

CHICKEN AND CORN SOUP

6¾ cups water, divided
2 pounds chicken pieces
1 medium yellow onion, thinly sliced
1 piece fresh ginger (about 1-inch square), pared and thinly sliced
6 whole peppercorns
1½ teaspoons salt, divided
1 or 2 sprigs fresh parsley
8 green onions
1 can (16 ounces) cream-style corn
2 teaspoons instant chicken bouillon granules
1 teaspoon sesame oil
½ teaspoon minced fresh ginger
⅛ teaspoon ground pepper
¼ cup cornstarch
2 egg whites
2 slices cooked ham (about 1 ounce each), cut into 1½-inch strips

1. Combine 6 cups of the water, the chicken pieces, yellow onion, sliced ginger, peppercorns, 1 teaspoon of the salt and the parsley in 5-quart stockpot or Dutch oven. Bring to a boil. Reduce heat to low; cover and simmer 1½ hours. Remove any scum or fat from top of stock.

2. Strain stock; return to stockpot. Cut meat from bones and shred with cleaver or knife to yield 1 cup shredded chicken.

3. Finely chop 4 of the green onions. Add chopped onions, corn, bouillon granules, sesame oil, minced ginger, pepper and remaining ½ teaspoon salt to stock. Bring to a boil.

4. Blend cornstarch with ½ cup of the remaining water in small cup. Stir into soup; cook and stir until soup thickens.

5. Beat egg whites and remaining ¼ cup water in small bowl. Stirring constantly, drizzle egg mixture slowly into soup. Stir in ham and shredded chicken.

6. Cut remaining 4 onions into thin slices. Pour soup into bowls; sprinkle with onions. *Makes 6 to 8 servings*

MEATS

BEEF WITH CASHEWS

1 pound beef rump steak, trimmed
4 tablespoons vegetable oil, divided
½ cup water
4 teaspoons cornstarch
4 teaspoons soy sauce
1 teaspoon sesame oil
1 teaspoon oyster sauce
1 teaspoon Chinese chili sauce
8 green onions, cut into 1-inch pieces
2 cloves garlic, crushed
1 piece fresh ginger (about 1 inch square),
    pared and finely chopped
⅔ cup unsalted, roasted cashews (about 3
    ounces)

1. Cut beef across the grain into thin slices about 2 inches long. Heat 2 tablespoons of the vegetable oil in wok or large skillet over high heat. Stir-fry ½ of beef until brown, 3 to 5 minutes. Remove and set aside. Repeat with remaining beef.

2. Combine water, cornstarch, soy sauce, sesame oil, oyster sauce and chili sauce in small bowl; mix well.

3. Heat remaining 2 tablespoons vegetable oil in wok over high heat. Add onions, garlic, ginger and cashews. Stir-fry 1 minute. Add meat and cornstarch mixture. Cook and stir until liquid boils and thickens. *Makes 4 servings*

SPICED PORK

3 tablespoons soy sauce, divided
2 tablespoons cornstarch
2 tablespoons dry sherry
1 teaspoon minced fresh ginger
½ teaspoon Chinese five-spice powder
⅛ teaspoon pepper
2 pounds boneless lean pork, cut into
    large pieces
  Vegetable oil for frying
¼ cup water
1 teaspoon instant chicken bouillon
    granules
  Chinese Mixed Pickled Vegetables (see
    page 140), optional

1. Combine 2 tablespoons of the soy sauce, the cornstarch, the sherry, ginger, five-spice powder and pepper in large bowl. Add pork, one piece at a time, turning to coat well. Cover and refrigerate 1 hour, stirring occasionally.

2. Heat oil in wok or large skillet to 375°F. Cook ½ of pork until brown and cooked through, 3 to 5 minutes. Drain on paper towels. Repeat with remaining pork. Cut pork into ¼- to ½-inch-wide slices. Transfer to serving dish; keep warm.

3. Combine water, bouillon granules and remaining 1 tablespoon soy sauce in small saucepan. Bring to a boil. Pour mixture over sliced pork. Garnish with Chinese Mixed Pickled Vegetables, if desired. *Makes 4 servings*

Beef with Cashews

Mu Shu Pork

MU SHU PORK

8 teaspoons soy sauce, divided
5 teaspoons dry sherry, divided
4 teaspoons cornstarch, divided
8 ounces boneless lean pork, cut into
    matchstick pieces
3 dried mushrooms
2 dried wood ears
7 teaspoons vegetable oil, divided
2 eggs, lightly beaten
1 tablespoon water
½ teaspoon sugar
1 teaspoon sesame oil
1 teaspoon minced fresh ginger
½ cup sliced bamboo shoots (½ of
    8-ounce can), cut into matchstick
    pieces
1 small carrot, shredded
½ cup chicken broth
2 cups bean sprouts (about 4 ounces)
2 green onions, cut into 1½-inch slivers
½ cup hoisin sauce
16 Mandarin Pancakes (see page 102)

1. For marinade, combine 2 teaspoons of the soy sauce, 2 teaspoons of the sherry and 1 teaspoon of the cornstarch in large bowl. Add pork and stir to coat. Let stand 30 minutes.

2. Place dried mushrooms and wood ears in small bowl and cover with hot water. Let stand 30 minutes. Drain and squeeze out excess water. Cut off and discard mushroom stems; cut caps into thin slices. Pinch out hard nobs from center of wood ears and discard; cut wood ears into thin strips.

3. Heat ½ teaspoon vegetable oil in small nonstick skillet over medium-high heat. Add ½ of eggs and tilt skillet to cover bottom. Cook just until egg is set. Loosen edges, turn omelet over and cook other side 5 seconds. Remove from skillet and repeat with another ½ teaspoon oil and remaining egg. When omelets are cool, cut in half. Stack halves and cut crosswise into ⅛-inch wide strips.

4. For sauce, combine remaining 6 teaspoons soy sauce, 3 teaspoons sherry and 3 teaspoons cornstarch in small bowl. Add the water, sugar and sesame oil; mix well.

5. Heat remaining 6 teaspoons vegetable oil in wok or large skillet over high heat. Add ginger and stir once. Add pork and stir-fry until meat is no longer pink, about 2 minutes. Add mushrooms, wood ears, bamboo shoots, carrot and chicken broth. Stir and toss 2 minutes. Add bean sprouts and onions; stir-fry 1 minute.

6. Stir cornstarch mixture; pour into wok and cook, stirring constantly, until sauce bubbles and thickens. Stir in omelet strips.

7. To serve, spread about 2 teaspoons hoisin sauce on each pancake. Spoon about 3 tablespoons pork mixture down center; roll up.
Makes 8 servings

MANDARIN PANCAKES

2 cups all-purpose flour
¾ cup boiling water
2 tablespoons sesame oil

1. Place flour in bowl and make a well in center. Pour in boiling water; stir with wooden spoon until dough looks like lumpy meal. Press into a ball. Knead dough until smooth and satiny on lightly floured work surface, about 5 minutes. Cover with clean towel and let rest 30 minutes.

2. Roll dough into 10-inch-long log. Cut into 10 equal pieces; keep covered.

3. Cut each piece of dough in half. Roll each half into a ball; flatten slightly. Roll each piece into a 3-inch circle on lightly floured work surface. Brush top of each with small amount of sesame oil. Stack 2 dough circles together, oil side in. Roll the pair together into a 6- to 7-inch circle. Repeat for remaining pieces of dough. (Keep uncooked pancakes covered while you roll out remaining dough.)

4. Heat nonstick skillet over medium-low heat. Cook pancakes, 1 pair at a time, turning every 30 seconds, until cakes are flecked with brown and feel dry, 2 to 3 minutes. (Be careful not to overcook; cakes become brittle.)

5. Remove from pan and separate into 2 pancakes while still hot. Stack on plate and keep covered while you cook remaining pancakes. Serve at once, refrigerate or freeze in resealable plastic bag. To reheat, wrap pancakes in clean towel (thaw completely, if using frozen). Steam over simmering water 5 minutes. Fold pancakes into quarters and arrange in serving basket.

Makes 20 pancakes

Satay Beef

SATAY BEEF

1 pound beef tenderloin, trimmed
5 tablespoons water, divided
1 teaspoon cornstarch
3½ teaspoons soy sauce, divided
1 to 2 teaspoons sesame oil
2 tablespoons vegetable oil
1 medium yellow onion, coarsely chopped
1 clove garlic, crushed
1 tablespoon dry sherry
1 tablespoon satay sauce
1 teaspoon curry powder
½ teaspoon sugar

1. Cut beef across the grain into thin slices. Flatten each slice by pressing with fingers.

2. Combine 3 tablespoons of the water, the cornstarch, 1½ teaspoons of the soy sauce and the sesame oil in medium bowl. Add beef; mix to coat well. Let stand 20 minutes.

3. Heat vegetable oil in wok or large skillet over high heat. Add ½ of beef, spreading out slices so they do not overlap. Cook slices on each side just until light brown, 2 to 3 minutes. Remove and set aside. Repeat with remaining meat.

4. Add onion and garlic to wok; stir-fry until onion is soft, about 3 minutes.

5. Combine remaining 2 tablespoons water, 2 teaspoons soy sauce, the sherry, satay sauce, curry powder and sugar in small cup. Add to wok; cook and stir until liquid boils. Return beef to wok; cook and stir until heated through. *Makes 4 servings*

Braised Lion's Head

BRAISED LION'S HEAD

MEATBALLS
1 pound lean ground pork
4 ounces shrimp, shelled, deveined and
    finely chopped
¼ cup sliced water chestnuts, finely
    chopped
1 teaspoon minced fresh ginger
1 green onion, finely chopped
1 tablespoon soy sauce
1 tablespoon dry sherry
½ teaspoon salt
½ teaspoon sugar
1 tablespoon cornstarch
1 egg, lightly beaten
2 tablespoons vegetable oil

SAUCE
1½ cups chicken broth
2 tablespoons soy sauce
½ teaspoon sugar
1 head napa cabbage (1½ to 2 pounds)
2 tablespoons cornstarch
3 tablespoons cold water
1 teaspoon sesame oil

1. For meatballs, combine all meatball ingredients except oil in large bowl; mix well. Divide mixture into 8 portions. Shape each portion into a ball.

2. Heat vegetable oil in wok or large nonstick skillet over medium-high heat. Brown meatballs, shaking or stirring occasionally so meatballs keep their shape, 6 to 8 minutes.

3. Transfer meatballs to 5-quart stockpot; discard drippings. Add chicken broth, soy sauce and sugar. Bring to a boil; reduce heat, cover and simmer 30 minutes.

4. While meatballs are cooking, core cabbage; cut base of leaves into 2-inch squares. Cut leafy tops in half. Place cabbage over meatballs. Cover and simmer 10 minutes more.

5. Using slotted spoon, transfer cabbage and meatballs to serving platter. Blend cornstarch and water in small cup. Stirring constantly, slowly add cornstarch mixture to pan juices; cook until slightly thickened. Stir in sesame oil. To serve, pour sauce over meatballs and cabbage. *Makes 4 to 6 servings*

BEEF WITH NOODLES

8 ounces Chinese-style thin egg noodles,
    cooked and drained
½ cup water
3 teaspoons soy sauce, divided
¼ teaspoon salt
2 teaspoons instant chicken bouillon
    granules
1 pound beef rump steak, trimmed
6 tablespoons vegetable oil, divided
6 green onions, diagonally sliced
1 piece fresh ginger (about 1 inch
    square), pared and thinly sliced
2 cloves garlic, crushed

1. Place a clean towel over wire cooling racks. Spread cooked noodles evenly over towel. Let dry about 3 hours.

2. Combine water, 2 teaspoons of the soy sauce, the salt and bouillon granules in small bowl. Cut beef across the grain into thin slices about 2 inches long.

3. Heat 4 tablespoons of the oil in wok or large skillet over high heat. Add noodles and stir-fry 3 minutes. Pour water mixture over noodles; toss until noodles are completely coated, about 2 minutes. Transfer noodles to serving plate; keep warm.

4. Heat remaining 2 tablespoons oil in wok over high heat. Add beef, onions, ginger, garlic and remaining 1 teaspoon soy sauce. Stir-fry until beef is cooked through, about 5 minutes. Spoon meat mixture over noodles. *Makes 4 servings*

SWEET AND SOUR PORK

¼ cup soy sauce
1½ tablespoons dry sherry
2 teaspoons sugar
1 egg yolk
2 pounds boneless lean pork, cut into
    1-inch pieces
10 tablespoons cornstarch, divided
3 cups plus 3 tablespoons vegetable oil,
    divided
1 can (20 ounces) pineapple chunks in
    syrup
¼ cup distilled white vinegar
3 tablespoons tomato sauce
1 cup water
1 large yellow onion, thinly sliced
8 green onions, diagonally cut into 1-inch
    pieces
1 red or green bell pepper, chopped
4 ounces fresh mushrooms, cut into
    quarters
2 stalks celery, diagonally cut into ½-inch
    slices
1 medium cucumber, seeded and cut into
    ¼-inch-wide pieces

1. For marinade, combine soy sauce, sherry, sugar and egg yolk in large bowl. Add pork; mix to coat well. Cover and refrigerate 1 hour, stirring occasionally.

2. Drain pork, reserving marinade. Place 8 tablespoons of the cornstarch into large bowl. Add pork pieces; toss to coat well. Heat 3 cups of the oil in wok or large skillet over high heat to 375°F. Add ½ of pork pieces; cook until brown, about 5 minutes. Drain on paper towels. Repeat with remaining pork.

3. Drain pineapple, reserving syrup. Combine the syrup, reserved soy sauce marinade, vinegar and tomato sauce in small bowl. Blend remaining 2 tablespoons cornstarch and the water in another small bowl.

4. Heat remaining 3 tablespoons oil in wok over high heat. Add all vegetables and stir-fry 3 minutes. Add pineapple syrup mixture and cornstarch mixture; cook and stir until sauce boils and thickens. Add pork and pineapple; stir-fry until heated through.

Makes 4 servings

BEEF WITH PEPPERS

1 ounce dried mushrooms
1 pound beef tenderloin, trimmed
2½ tablespoons vegetable oil
1 clove garlic, crushed
¼ teaspoon Chinese five-spice powder
2 small yellow onions, cut into wedges
1 green bell pepper, thinly sliced
1 red bell pepper, thinly sliced
¼ cup water
1 tablespoon soy sauce
1 teaspoon cornstarch
1 teaspoon instant beef bouillon granules
1 teaspoon sesame oil

1. Place mushrooms in bowl and cover with hot water. Let stand 30 minutes. Drain and squeeze out excess water. Remove and discard stems; slice caps into thin strips.

2. Cut beef into thin slices 1 inch long.

3. Heat vegetable oil in wok or large skillet over high heat. Add garlic and five spice powder; stir-fry 15 seconds. Add beef and stir-fry until brown, about 5 minutes. Add onions; stir-fry 2 minutes. Add mushrooms and peppers; stir-fry until peppers are crisp-tender, about 2 minutes.

4. Combine remaining ingredients in small bowl. Stir into wok. Cook and stir until liquid boils and thickens. *Makes 4 servings*

Sweet and Sour Pork

Mongolian Lamb

MONGOLIAN LAMB

SESAME SAUCE

1 tablespoon sesame seeds
¼ cup soy sauce
1 tablespoon dry sherry
1 tablespoon red wine vinegar
1½ teaspoons sugar
1 clove garlic, minced
1 green onion, minced
½ teaspoon sesame oil

LAMB

1 pound boneless lean lamb (leg or
     shoulder)
2 small leeks, cut into 2-inch slivers
4 green onions, cut into 2-inch slivers
2 medium carrots, shredded
1 medium zucchini, shredded
1 red pepper, cut into matchstick pieces
1 green bell pepper, cut into matchstick
     pieces
½ small head napa cabbage, thinly sliced
1 cup bean sprouts
4 tablespoons vegetable oil, divided
4 slices pared fresh ginger, divided
     Chili oil, optional

1. For sauce, place sesame seeds in small frying pan. Shake over medium heat until seeds begin to pop and turn golden, about 2 minutes. Let cool. Crush seeds with mortar and pestle (or place on cutting board and crush with a rolling pin; scrape up sesame paste with knife) and transfer to small serving bowl. Add remaining sauce ingredients; mix well.

2. For lamb, slice meat across the grain into strips ¼ inch thick and 2 inches long.

3. Arrange meat and vegetables on large platter. Have Sesame Sauce, vegetable oil, ginger and chili oil near cooking area.

4. At serving time, heat electric griddle or wok to 350°F. Cook one serving at a time. For each serving, heat 1 tablespoon vegetable oil; add 1 slice ginger and cook 30 seconds; discard ginger. Add ½ cup meat strips; stir-fry until lightly browned, about 1 minute. Add 2 cups assorted vegetables; stir-fry 1 minute. Drizzle with 2 tablespoons Sesame Sauce; stir-fry 30 seconds. Season with a few drops chili oil, if desired. Repeat for remaining servings.   *Makes 4 servings*

HONEY–GLAZED SPARERIBS

1 side pork spareribs (about 2 pounds)
¼ cup plus 1 tablespoon soy sauce,
    divided
3 tablespoons hoisin sauce
3 tablespoons dry sherry, divided
1 tablespoon sugar
1 teaspoon minced fresh ginger
2 cloves garlic, minced
¼ teaspoon Chinese five-spice powder
2 tablespoons honey
1 tablespoon cider vinegar
    Green Onion Curls (see page 84) for
    garnish

1. Have your butcher cut ribs down length of slab into 2 pieces so that each half is 2 to 3 inches wide. Cut between bones to make 6-inch pieces. Trim excess fat. Place ribs in heavy plastic bag.

2. For marinade, combine ¼ cup of the soy sauce, the hoisin sauce, 2 tablespoons of the sherry, the sugar, ginger, garlic and five-spice powder in small bowl; mix well. Pour marinade over ribs. Seal bag tightly and place in large bowl. Refrigerate 8 hours or overnight, turning bag occasionally.

3. Foil-line a large baking pan. Place rack in pan and place ribs on rack (reserve marinade). Bake in preheated 350°F oven 30 minutes. Turn ribs over, brush with marinade and bake until ribs are tender when pierced with fork, about 40 minutes more.

4. For glaze, combine honey, vinegar, remaining 1 tablespoon soy sauce and 1 tablespoon sherry in small bowl; mix well. Brush ½ of mixture over ribs; place under broiler 4 to 6 inches from heat source and broil until ribs are glazed, 2 to 3 minutes. Turn ribs over, brush with remaining honey mixture and broil until glazed. Cut into serving-size pieces. Garnish with Green Onion Curls, if desired. *Makes about 4 servings*

Honey-Glazed Spareribs

GINGER BEEF

2½ tablespoons distilled white vinegar
2 teaspoons sugar
½ teaspoon salt
4 ounces fresh ginger, pared and thinly sliced
1 pound beef tenderloin, trimmed
2 tablespoons dry sherry
2 teaspoons cornstarch
1 teaspoon soy sauce
3 tablespoons vegetable oil, divided
1 large green bell pepper, cut into 1-inch pieces
6 green onions, cut into 1-inch pieces
1 red chili pepper, cut into thin slices, for garnish

1. Combine vinegar, sugar and salt in small bowl; stir until sugar dissolves. Add ginger. Let stand 20 to 30 minutes, stirring occasionally.

2. Cut beef across the grain into thin slices about 1½-inches long. Combine sherry, cornstarch and soy sauce in medium bowl. Add beef; stir to coat well. Let stand 20 minutes, stirring occasionally. Drain beef, reserving marinade.

3. Heat 2 tablespoons of the oil in wok or large skillet over high heat. Add ⅓ of beef, spreading slices out so they do not overlap. Cook slices on each side just until light brown, 2 to 3 minutes. Remove and set aside. Repeat twice with remaining beef.

4. Heat remaining 1 tablespoon oil in wok. Add green pepper, onions, ginger mixture and reserved marinade. Stir-fry until vegetables are crisp-tender, 2 to 3 minutes. Return beef to wok. Cook and stir until heated through. Garnish with chili pepper, if desired.   *Makes 4 servings*

TWO–ONION PORK SHREDS

½ teaspoon Szechuan peppercorns
4 teaspoons soy sauce, divided
4 teaspoons dry sherry, divided
7½ teaspoons vegetable oil, divided
1 teaspoon cornstarch
8 ounces boneless lean pork
2 teaspoons red wine vinegar
½ teaspoon sugar
2 cloves garlic, crushed
½ small yellow onion, cut into ¼-inch slices
8 green onions, cut into 2-inch pieces
½ teaspoon sesame oil

1. For marinade, place peppercorns in small skillet. Shake over medium-low heat, shaking skillet often, until fragrant, about 2 minutes. Let cool. Crush peppercorns with mortar and pestle (or place between paper towels and crush with a hammer).* Transfer to medium bowl. Add 2 teaspoons of the soy sauce, 2 teaspoons of the sherry, 1½ teaspoons of the vegetable oil and the cornstarch; mix well.

2. Cut pork into ⅛-inch-thick slices, then cut into 2×½-inch pieces. Add to marinade; stir to coat. Let stand 30 minutes. Combine remaining 2 teaspoons soy sauce, 2 teaspoons sherry, the vinegar and sugar in small bowl; mix well.

3. Heat remaining 6 teaspoons vegetable oil in wok or large skillet over high heat. Add garlic and stir once. Add pork and stir-fry until meat is no longer pink, about 2 minutes. Add yellow onion and stir-fry 1 minute; add green onion and stir-fry 30 seconds. Add soy-vinegar mixture and cook 30 seconds. Stir in sesame oil.   *Makes 2 to 3 servings*

*Note: Szechuan peppercorns are deceptively potent. Wear rubber or plastic gloves when crushing them and do not touch your eyes or lips when handling.

POULTRY

ALMOND CHICKEN

1½ cups water
4 tablespoons dry sherry, divided
2½ tablespoons cornstarch, divided
4 teaspoons soy sauce
1 teaspoon instant chicken bouillon
    granules
1 egg white
½ teaspoon salt
4 whole boneless, skinless chicken
    breasts, cut into 1-inch pieces
    Vegetable oil for frying
½ cup blanched whole almonds (about 3
    ounces)
1 large carrot, diced
1 teaspoon minced fresh ginger
6 green onions, cut into 1-inch pieces
3 stalks celery, diagonally cut into ½-inch
    pieces
8 fresh mushrooms, sliced
½ cup sliced bamboo shoots (½ of
    8-ounce can), drained

1. Combine water, 2 tablespoons of the sherry, 1½ tablespoons of the cornstarch, the soy sauce and bouillon granules in small saucepan. Cook and stir over medium heat until mixture boils and thickens, about 5 minutes. Keep warm.

2. Combine remaining 2 tablespoons sherry, 1 tablespoon cornstarch, egg white and salt in medium bowl. Add chicken pieces; stir to coat well.

3. Heat oil in wok or large skillet over high heat to 375°F. Add chicken pieces, one at a time (cook only ⅓ of the pieces at a time), and cook until light brown, 3 to 5 minutes. Drain on paper towels. Repeat with remaining chicken.

4. Remove all but 2 tablespoons oil from wok. Add almonds and stir-fry until golden, about 2 minutes; drain.

5. Add carrot and ginger; stir-fry 1 minute. Add all remaining vegetables; stir-fry until crisp-tender, about 3 minutes. Stir in chicken, almonds and sauce; cook and stir until heated through.
Makes 4 to 6 servings

Almond Chicken

Kung Pao Chicken

KUNG PAO CHICKEN

5 teaspoons soy sauce, divided
5 teaspoons dry sherry, divided
3½ teaspoons cornstarch, divided
¼ teaspoon salt
3 boneless, skinless chicken breast
   halves, cut into bite-size pieces
1 tablespoon red wine vinegar
2 tablespoons chicken broth or water
1½ teaspoons sugar
3 tablespoons vegetable oil, divided
⅓ cup salted peanuts
6 to 8 small dried hot chili peppers
1½ teaspoons minced fresh ginger
2 green onions, cut into 1½-inch pieces

1. For marinade, combine 2 teaspoons of the soy sauce, 2 teaspoons of the sherry, 2 teaspoons of the cornstarch and the salt in large bowl; mix well. Add chicken; stir to coat well. Let stand 30 minutes.

2. Combine remaining 3 teaspoons soy sauce, 3 teaspoons sherry, the vinegar, chicken broth, sugar and remaining 1½ teaspoons cornstarch in small bowl; mix well and set aside.

3. Heat 1 tablespoon of the oil in wok or large skillet over medium heat. Add peanuts and cook until golden. Remove and set aside.

4. Heat remaining 2 tablespoons oil in wok over medium heat. Add chili peppers and stir-fry until peppers just begin to char, about 1 minute. Increase heat to high. Add chicken and stir-fry 2 minutes. Add ginger; stir-fry until chicken is cooked through, about 1 minute more. Add onions and peanuts to wok. Stir cornstarch mixture and add to wok; cook and stir until sauce boils and thickens. *Makes 3 servings*

HOW TO CUT CHICKEN CHINESE-STYLE

Recipes for Chinese chicken dishes often instruct that chicken be cut into serving-size pieces. These pieces should be smaller than chicken pieces generally are cut. Here are the directions for cutting a whole chicken Chinese-style. A cleaver is the best utensil for chopping a chicken, although a sharp knife or poultry shears may be used.

1. Place chicken breast-side up on a heavy cutting board. Cut in half lengthwise, cutting slightly to one side of the breast bone and the backbone. Cut completely through the chicken to make two pieces. Remove and discard backbone, if desired.

2. Pull each leg up slightly from the breast section. Cut through the ball and socket joint to remove each leg.

3. Cut through the knee joint of each leg to separate into a drumstick and thigh. Pull each wing away from breast and cut through the joint next to the breast.

4. Cut each drumstick, thigh and breast piece crosswise into three pieces, cutting completely through bones. Cut each wing into two pieces. *Makes 22 small serving-size pieces*

Step 1

Step 2

Step 3

Step 4

HOISIN CHICKEN

1 broiler/fryer chicken (3 to 4 pounds)
½ cup plus 1 tablespoon cornstarch, divided
  Vegetable oil for frying
2 teaspoons grated fresh ginger
2 medium yellow onions, chopped
8 ounces fresh broccoli, cut into 1-inch pieces
1 red or green bell pepper, chopped
2 cans (4 ounces each) whole button mushrooms, drained
1 cup water
3 tablespoons dry sherry
3 tablespoons cider vinegar
3 tablespoons hoisin sauce
4 teaspoons soy sauce
2 teaspoons instant chicken bouillon granules

1. Rinse chicken and cut into small serving-size pieces (page 115). Place ½ cup of the cornstarch in large bowl. Add chicken pieces and toss to coat well.

2. Heat oil in wok or large skillet over high heat to 375°F. Add chicken pieces, one at a time (cook only about ⅓ of the chicken pieces at a time), and cook until golden and cooked through, about 5 minutes. Drain on paper towels. Repeat with remaining chicken.

3. Remove all but 2 tablespoons oil from wok. Add ginger and stir-fry 1 minute. Add onions; stir-fry 1 minute. Add broccoli, red pepper and mushrooms; stir-fry 2 minutes.

4. Combine remaining ingredients and remaining 1 tablespoon cornstarch in small bowl. Add to wok. Cook and stir until sauce boils and turns translucent. Return chicken to wok. Cook and stir until chicken is heated through, about 2 minutes.

Makes 6 servings

CHICKEN WITH MANGOES

1 cup all-purpose flour
1¾ cups water, divided
½ teaspoon salt
¼ teaspoon baking powder
3 whole boneless, skinless chicken breasts, cut into thin strips
  Vegetable oil for frying
1 piece fresh ginger (2×1 inch), pared and thinly sliced
3 tablespoons distilled white vinegar
3 tablespoons dry sherry
4 teaspoons soy sauce
2 teaspoons sugar
2 teaspoons cornstarch
2 teaspoons instant chicken bouillon granules
1 teaspoon sesame oil
8 green onions, cut into ½-inch pieces
1 can (15 ounces) mangoes, drained and cut into ½-inch strips
  Vermicelli (see page 148), cooked and drained, optional

1. Combine flour, 1 cup of the water, the salt and baking powder in medium bowl. Beat with whisk until blended. Let stand 15 minutes. Add chicken; stir to coat well.

2. Heat vegetable oil in wok or large skillet to 375°F. Add chicken, one strip at a time (cook only about ¼ of the chicken strips at a time), and cook until golden, 3 to 5 minutes. Drain on paper towels. Repeat with remaining chicken.

3. Remove all but 1 tablespoon oil from wok. Reduce heat to medium. Add ginger; stir-fry until light brown, about 2 minutes.

4. Combine remaining ¾ cup water, the vinegar, sherry, soy sauce, sugar, cornstarch, bouillon granules and sesame oil in small bowl. Slowly pour into wok. Cook and stir until sauce boils. Add onions, reduce heat and simmer 3 minutes. Stir chicken and mangoes into wok. Cook and stir 2 minutes. Serve with Vermicelli, if desired.

Makes 4 to 6 servings

Hoisin Chicken

Lemon Chicken

LEMON CHICKEN

CHICKEN
- 4 whole boneless, skinless chicken breasts
- ½ cup cornstarch
- ½ teaspoon salt
- ⅛ teaspoon pepper
- ¼ cup water
- 4 egg yolks, lightly beaten
  Vegetable oil for frying
- 4 green onions, sliced

LEMON SAUCE
- 1½ cups water
- ½ cup lemon juice
- 3½ tablespoons brown sugar
- 3 tablespoons cornstarch
- 3 tablespoons honey
- 2 teaspoons instant chicken bouillon granules
- 1 teaspoon minced fresh ginger

1. Cut chicken breasts in half. Pound with mallet or rolling pin to flatten slightly.

2. Combine cornstarch, salt and pepper in small bowl. Gradually blend in water and egg yolks.

3. Heat oil in wok or large skillet over high heat to 375°F. Dip chicken breasts, one at a time, into cornstarch-egg yolk mixture. Cook chicken breasts, two at a time, until golden, about 5 minutes. Drain on paper towels. Keep warm while cooking remaining chicken.

4. Cut each breast into three or four pieces and arrange on serving plate. Sprinkle with onions.

5. For sauce, combine all sauce ingredients in medium saucepan; mix well. Cook over medium heat, stirring constantly, until sauce boils and thickens, about 5 minutes. Pour over chicken.

Makes 4 to 6 servings

GINGER GREEN ONION CHICKEN

- 1 broiler/fryer chicken (3 to 4 pounds)
- 1 piece fresh ginger (2×1 inch), pared and thinly sliced
- 1¼ teaspoons salt, divided
- ½ teaspoon pepper, divided
- ⅓ cup vegetable oil
- 8 green onions, finely chopped
- 3 tablespoons minced fresh ginger
- 2 teaspoons distilled white vinegar
- 1 teaspoon soy sauce
  Steamed Rice (see page 151), optional

1. Rinse chicken and place in large stockpot or Dutch oven. Add sliced ginger, 1 teaspoon of the salt, ¼ teaspoon of the pepper and enough water to cover chicken. Cover and bring to a boil over high heat. Reduce heat and simmer until tender, about 40 minutes. Let stand until cool.

2. Strain stock and refrigerate or freeze for another use. Refrigerate chicken until cold, then cut into small serving-size pieces (see page 115).

3. Combine remaining ¼ teaspoon salt, ¼ teaspoon pepper, oil, onions, ginger, vinegar and soy sauce in jar with tight-fitting lid. Shake to mix well. Refrigerate 1 to 2 hours.

4. Place chicken in serving bowl. Shake onion-ginger mixture and pour over chicken. Serve with Steamed Rice, if desired.

Makes 4 to 6 servings

CHICKEN CHOW MEIN

Fried Noodles (see page 154)
2½ tablespoons dry sherry, divided
2 tablespoons soy sauce, divided
3 teaspoons cornstarch, divided
2 whole boneless, skinless chicken
    breasts, cut into 1-inch pieces
8 ounces boneless lean pork, cut into
    1-inch pieces
½ cup water
2 teaspoons instant chicken bouillon
    granules
2 tablespoons vegetable oil
1 piece fresh ginger (1 inch square),
    pared and finely chopped
1 clove garlic, crushed
8 ounces shelled, deveined shrimp
2 medium yellow onions, chopped
1 red or green bell pepper, thinly sliced
2 stalks celery, diagonally cut into 1-inch
    slices
8 green onions, chopped
4 ounces cabbage, shredded

1. Prepare Fried Noodles; set aside.

2. Blend ½ tablespoon of the sherry, ½ tablespoon of the soy sauce and 1 teaspoon of the cornstarch in large bowl. Add chicken and pork; toss to coat well. Cover and refrigerate 1 hour.

3. Combine water, bouillon granules, remaining 2 teaspoons cornstarch, 2 tablespoons sherry and 1½ tablespoons soy sauce in small bowl; set aside. Heat oil in wok or large skillet over high heat. Add ginger and garlic and stir-fry 1 minute. Add chicken and pork; stir-fry until pork is no longer pink, about 5 minutes. Add shrimp; stir-fry until shrimp turn pink, about 3 minutes.

4. Add all vegetables to wok. Stir-fry until vegetables are crisp-tender, 3 to 5 minutes. Add bouillon-soy sauce mixture to wok. Cook and stir until sauce boils and thickens, then cook and stir 1 minute more.

5. Arrange Fried Noodles on serving plate; spoon chow mein over noodles.
Makes 6 servings

SESAME CHICKEN SALAD

1 tablespoon sesame seeds
3 whole chicken breasts
6 cups water
2 tablespoons soy sauce, divided
½ teaspoon salt
½ teaspoon Chinese five-spice powder
3 stalks celery
1 tablespoon sesame oil
1 tablespoon vegetable oil
¼ teaspoon ground ginger
⅛ teaspoon pepper

1. Sprinkle sesame seeds into small shallow baking pan. Bake in preheated 350°F oven until golden, 5 to 8 minutes.

2. Combine chicken, water, 1 tablespoon of the soy sauce, the salt and five-spice powder in 3- or 4-quart saucepan. Cover and bring to a boil. Reduce heat and simmer 15 to 20 minutes. Remove from heat. Let stand until chicken is cool enough to handle, about 1 hour.

3. Using slotted spoon, remove chicken and drain (reserve broth). Remove and discard bones. Cut meat into ½-inch wide slices.

4. Cut celery into diagonal slices. Bring reserved cooking broth back to boil. Add celery and cook until crisp-tender, 1 to 2 minutes. Using slotted spoon, remove celery and drain.

5. Combine remaining 1 tablespoon soy sauce, sesame and vegetable oils, ginger and pepper in large bowl. Add chicken and celery; toss to coat well. Transfer to serving bowl. Sprinkle with toasted sesame seeds.
Makes 4 servings

Chicken Chow Mein

DUCK WITH PINEAPPLE

1 ready-to-cook duck (4 to 5 pounds)
1¼ cups water, divided
6 tablespoons dry sherry, divided
4½ tablespoons distilled white vinegar, divided
4½ tablespoons soy sauce, divided
4 tablespoons American-style barbecue sauce, divided
¼ teaspoon Chinese five-spice powder
1 small ripe pineapple
1 tablespoon cornstarch
2 tablespoons vegetable oil
2 teaspoons minced fresh ginger
1 clove garlic, crushed
4 green onions, diagonally cut into thin slices
Green Onion Curls (see page 84), for garnish

1. Rinse duck and place on wire rack in large baking pan. Combine ½ cup of the water, 3 tablespoons *each* of the sherry, vinegar, soy sauce and barbecue sauce, and the ¼ teaspoon five-spice powder in medium bowl; mix well. Pour mixture over duck. Roast duck, uncovered, in preheated 425°F oven, basting and turning often, until light brown, about 20 minutes. Reduce oven temperature to 350°F and roast duck, basting and turning often, 1 hour more. Remove duck from oven; cool completely.

2. Cut duck in half. Remove and discard backbone. Cut duck into small serving-size pieces (see page 51).

3. Twist crown from pineapple. Cut pineapple lengthwise into quarters. Using curved knife, remove fruit from shells. Trim off core and cut fruit into ¼-inch slices.

4. Combine remaining ¾ cup water, 3 tablespoons sherry, 1½ tablespoons *each* vinegar and soy sauce, 1 tablespoon barbecue sauce and the cornstarch in small bowl. Heat oil in wok or large skillet over high heat. Add ginger and garlic and stir-fry 1 minute. Add duck pieces; stir-fry until duck is hot, 3 to 4 minutes. Stir water mixture and pour over duck; cook and stir until sauce boils. Add pineapple slices and onions. Cook and stir until pineapple is hot, about 2 minutes more. Garnish with Green Onion Curls, if desired. *Makes 6 servings*

MARINATED CHICKEN WINGS

3 tablespoons soy sauce
3 tablespoons dry sherry
2 tablespoons brown sugar
1 teaspoon grated fresh ginger
2 cloves garlic, crushed
6 green onions, diagonally cut into thin slices
1½ pounds chicken wings, tips cut off
2 tablespoons vegetable oil
1 can (8 ounces) sliced bamboo shoots, drained
4 teaspoons cornstarch
¾ cup water
1 teaspoon instant chicken bouillon granules

1. For marinade, combine soy sauce, sherry, sugar, ginger and garlic in large bowl. Add onions and chicken; toss to coat well. Cover and refrigerate 1 hour, stirring occasionally.

2. Heat oil in wok or large skillet over high heat. Add bamboo shoots and stir-fry 2 minutes. Remove and set aside.

3. Drain chicken and onions, reserving marinade. Add chicken and onions to wok; stir-fry over medium-high heat until chicken is brown, about 5 minutes. Reduce heat to low. Cook until chicken is tender, 15 to 20 minutes.

4. Blend cornstarch and water in small bowl. Stir in bouillon granules and reserved marinade. Add cornstarch mixture to wok. Cook over high heat until liquid boils and thickens. Stir in bamboo shoots. Cook and stir 2 minutes. *Makes 4 servings*

Chinese Chicken Salad

CHINESE CHICKEN SALAD

2 whole chicken breasts
4 cups water
1 tablespoon dry sherry
2 slices pared fresh ginger
2 whole green onions
¼ cup prepared Chinese plum sauce
2 tablespoons distilled white vinegar
1 tablespoon vegetable oil
1 tablespoon sesame oil
1½ teaspoons soy sauce
1½ tablespoons sugar
1 teaspoon dry mustard
3 tablespoons slivered almonds
2 tablespoons sesame seeds
4 cups shredded iceberg lettuce
1 small carrot, shredded
1½ cups bean sprouts (about 3 ounces)
3 green onions, cut into 1½-inch slivers
¼ cup cilantro leaves (Chinese parsley)
   Bean threads or Vermicelli (page 148),
    cooked and drained

1. Combine chicken, water, sherry, ginger and whole green onions in 3-quart saucepan. Bring to a boil; reduce heat, cover and simmer 20 minutes. Remove from heat. Let stand until cool.

2. Strain stock and refrigerate or freeze for another use. Remove and discard skin and bones from chicken. Pull meat into long shreds.

3. For dressing, combine plum sauce, vinegar, vegetable and sesame oils, soy sauce, sugar and mustard in small bowl; mix well.

4. Place almonds in small dry skillet. Shake over medium heat until golden and fragrant, about 3 minutes. Transfer to large salad bowl. Toast sesame seeds in same skillet until seeds are golden and begin to pop, about 2 minutes. Add sesame seeds to almonds.

5. Add lettuce, carrot, bean sprouts, green onion slivers, cilantro, cooked chicken and dressing. Toss to coat evenly. Add bean threads and toss to mix well. *Makes 6 to 8 servings*

Asparagus Chicken with Black Bean Sauce

ASPARAGUS CHICKEN WITH BLACK BEAN SAUCE

1 tablespoon dry sherry
4 teaspoons soy sauce, divided
5 teaspoons cornstarch, divided
1 teaspoon sesame oil
3 boneless, skinless chicken breast
    halves, cut into bite-size pieces
1 tablespoon fermented, salted black
    beans
1 teaspoon minced fresh ginger
1 clove garlic, minced
½ cup chicken broth
1 tablespoon oyster sauce
3 tablespoons vegetable oil, divided
1 pound fresh asparagus spears, trimmed
    and diagonally cut into 1-inch pieces
1 medium yellow onion, cut into 8 wedges
    and separated
2 tablespoons water

1. For marinade, combine sherry, 2 teaspoons of the soy sauce, 2 teaspoons of the cornstarch and the sesame oil in large bowl; mix well. Add chicken and stir to coat well. Let stand 30 minutes.

2. Place black beans in sieve and rinse under cold running water. Coarsely chop beans. Combine beans, ginger and garlic; finely chop all three together. Combine chicken broth, remaining 2 teaspoons soy sauce, the oyster sauce and the remaining 3 teaspoons cornstarch in small bowl; mix well and set aside.

3. Heat 2 tablespoons of the vegetable oil in wok or large skillet over high heat. Add chicken and stir-fry until chicken turns opaque, about 3 minutes. Remove and set aside.

4. Heat remaining 1 tablespoon vegetable oil in wok. Add asparagus and onion and stir-fry 30 seconds. Add water; cover and cook, stirring occasionally, until asparagus is crisp-tender, about 2 minutes. Return chicken to wok.

5. Stir chicken broth mixture and add to wok with bean mixture; cook and stir until sauce boils and thickens.

Makes 3 to 4 servings

CHICKEN WITH WATER CHESTNUTS

1 ounce dried mushrooms
⅔ cup water
4 teaspoons cornstarch
1 tablespoon instant chicken bouillon
    granules
1 tablespoon dry sherry
1 tablespoon soy sauce
1 tablespoon oyster sauce
1½ cups vegetable oil
2 whole boneless, skinless chicken
    breasts, cut into 1-inch pieces
3 stalks celery, diagonally cut into ½-inch
    slices
1 red or green bell pepper, thinly sliced
1 medium yellow onion, cut into wedges
1 can (8 ounces) water chestnuts, drained
    and cut into halves
8 ounces bean sprouts
1 piece (about 1 inch square) fresh
    ginger, pared and thinly sliced

1. Place mushrooms in medium bowl and cover with hot water. Let stand 30 minutes. Drain and squeeze out excess water. Remove and discard stems; cut caps into halves.

2. Combine ⅔ cup water, cornstarch, bouillon granules, sherry, soy sauce and oyster sauce in small bowl; mix well.

3. Heat oil in wok or large skillet over high heat to 375°F. Add chicken pieces, one at a time (cook only ½ of the pieces at a time), and cook until golden, about 5 minutes. Drain on paper towels.

4. Remove all but 2 tablespoons oil from wok. Add mushrooms, celery, red pepper, onion, water chestnuts, bean sprouts, ginger and chicken to wok. Toss to mix well.

5. Stir water mixture and add to wok. Cook and stir until vegetables are crisp-tender, 3 to 5 minutes. *Makes 4 servings*

TEA SMOKED CHICKEN

1 teaspoon Szechuan peppercorns
2 tablespoons dry sherry
2 tablespoons soy sauce
½ teaspoon granulated sugar
6 thin slices pared fresh ginger
2 green onions, cut into 2-inch pieces
1 teaspoon salt
1 broiler/fryer chicken (3 to 4 pounds)
⅓ cup black tea leaves
3 tablespoons brown sugar
⅓ cup long-grain rice
1 strip dried tangerine peel (about
   2 inches long) or 1 teaspoon grated
   orange peel
Mandarin Pancakes (page 102)
Prepared plum sauce or hoisin sauce
4 green onions, cut into 2-inch slivers

1. For marinade, crush peppercorns with mortar and pestle (or place between paper towels and crush with a hammer). Combine crushed peppercorns, sherry, soy sauce, granulated sugar, ginger, onion pieces and salt. Rub chicken inside and out with marinade.* Cover and refrigerate 8 hours or overnight.

2. Place chicken breast-side up on rack in large stockpot. Pour in 1½ inches water. Cover, bring to a boil, and steam until meat near thigh bone is no longer pink, about 45 to 50 minutes. Let stand until cool enough to handle. Lift chicken from rack and drain juices from cavity.

3. Line a large wok and its lid with foil. (Do not use an electric wok with nonstick finish.) For smoking, place tea leaves, brown sugar, rice and tangerine peel in bottom of foil-lined wok; mix well. Set rack on top of mixture in wok. Place chicken breast-side up on rack. Cover with foil-lined lid.

4. Cook over high heat 2 minutes. Turn off heat and leave covered 5 minutes. Repeat 2 more times. After final smoking, let stand, covered, to allow smoke to subside, about 30 minutes. Discard smoking mixture.

5. Slice chicken from bones and arrange on serving platter. Serve 1 or 2 chicken slices in Mandarin Pancake; top with plum sauce and slivered onions.   *Makes 6 to 8 servings*

*Note: Szechuan peppercorns are deceptively potent. Wear rubber or plastic gloves when rubbing chicken with marinade and do not touch your eyes or lips when handling peppercorns or marinade.

Tea Smoked Chicken

HONEYED CHICKEN AND PINEAPPLE

1 broiler/fryer chicken (3 to 4 pounds)
½ cup plus 2 teaspoons cornstarch, divided
  Vegetable oil for frying
2 teaspoons minced fresh ginger
1 clove garlic, crushed
1 can (20 ounces) pineapple chunks, drained
1 red or green bell pepper, thinly sliced
1½ cups water
1½ tablespoons honey
1 tablespoon instant chicken bouillon granules
1 teaspoon sesame oil
4 green onions, thinly sliced

1. Rinse chicken and cut into small serving-size pieces (see page 115). Place ½ cup of the cornstarch in large bowl. Add chicken pieces and toss to coat well.

2. Heat oil in wok or large skillet over high heat to 375°F. Add chicken pieces, one at a time (cook only ⅓ of the pieces at a time), and cook until golden and cooked through, about 5 minutes. Drain on paper towels. Repeat with remaining chicken.

3. Remove all but 2 tablespoons oil from wok. Add ginger and garlic and stir-fry 1 minute. Add pineapple and red pepper; stir-fry 2 minutes. Remove and set aside.

4. Combine water and remaining 2 teaspoons cornstarch in small bowl. Blend in honey, bouillon granules and sesame oil. Pour mixture into wok; cook and stir until sauce boils and thickens. Return chicken and pineapple-pepper mixture to wok; cook and stir until heated through. Add green onions; cook and stir 1 minute more. *Makes 4 servings*

SEAFOOD

CRAB–STUFFED SHRIMP

SAUCE
  2 tablespoons vegetable oil
  1 small yellow onion, finely chopped
  1 teaspoon curry powder
1½ tablespoons dry sherry
  1 tablespoon satay sauce
  1 teaspoon sugar
  2 teaspoons soy sauce
  ¼ cup cream or milk

SHRIMP
  2 egg whites
  4 teaspoons cornstarch
  1 tablespoon dry sherry
  1 tablespoon soy sauce
  2 cans (6½ ounces each) crab meat,
      drained and flaked
  8 green onions, finely chopped
  2 stalks celery, finely chopped
1½ pounds large shrimp, shelled and
      deveined
  ½ cup all-purpose flour
  3 eggs
  3 tablespoons milk
  2 to 3 cups soft bread crumbs
      (8 to 10 bread slices)
    Vegetable oil for frying

1. For sauce, heat 2 tablespoons oil in small saucepan over medium heat. Add onion and cook until onion is transparent, about 3 minutes. Add curry powder; cook and stir 1 minute. Add sherry, satay sauce, sugar and soy sauce; cook and stir 2 minutes. Stir in cream; bring to a boil. Boil 2 minutes. Keep warm.

2. For shrimp, blend egg whites, cornstarch, sherry and soy sauce in medium bowl. Add crab meat, onions and celery; mix well.

3. Cut deep slit into but not through back of each shrimp. Flatten shrimp by pounding gently with mallet or rolling pin. Spoon crab mixture onto each shrimp and press with back of spoon or small spatula.

4. Coat each shrimp lightly with flour. Beat eggs and milk with fork in shallow bowl until blended. Place each shrimp stuffed-side up in egg mixture, then spoon mixture over shrimp to cover completely. Coat each shrimp completely with bread crumbs, pressing crumbs lightly onto shrimp. Place shrimp in single layer on cookie sheets or plates. Refrigerate 30 minutes.

5. Heat oil in wok or large skillet over high heat to 375°F. Cook 4 or 5 shrimp at a time until golden, about 3 minutes. Drain on paper towels. Serve with warm sauce.　*Makes 4 servings*

Crab-Stuffed Shrimp

FRAGRANT BRAISED OYSTERS

1 jar (10 or 12 ounces) shucked oysters,
    drained
2 cups plus 1 tablespoon water, divided
½ teaspoon salt
¼ cup chicken broth
1 tablespoon dry sherry
1 tablespoon oyster sauce
1 teaspoon cornstarch
¼ teaspoon sugar
2 tablespoons vegetable oil, divided
3 slices (about ½ inch each) pared fresh
    ginger, cut into thin slivers
½ small yellow onion, cut into wedges and
    separated
3 green onions, cut into 2-inch pieces

1. If oysters are large, cut into bite-size pieces. In 2-quart saucepan, bring 2 cups of the water and the salt to a boil. Add oysters. Turn off heat and let stand 30 seconds. Drain, rinse under cold running water and drain again.

2. Combine chicken broth, sherry, oyster sauce, remaining 1 tablespoon water, the cornstarch and sugar in small bowl; mix well.

3. Heat 1 tablespoon of the oil in wok or large skillet over high heat. Add ginger and yellow onion; stir-fry 1 minute. Add green onions; stir-fry 30 seconds. Remove and set aside.

4. Heat remaining 1 tablespoon oil in wok. Add blanched oysters and stir-fry 2 minutes. Return ginger and onions to wok. Stir cornstarch mixture and add to wok. Cook and stir until sauce boils and thickens. *Makes 2 to 3 servings*

Fragrant Braised Oysters

CRAB IN GINGER SAUCE

2 ready-to-cook, whole hard-shell crabs
¾ cup water, divided
2½ tablespoons dry sherry
1 teaspoon sugar
1 teaspoon instant chicken bouillon
    granules
2 teaspoons soy sauce
2 teaspoons cornstarch
2 tablespoons vegetable oil
½ teaspoon sesame oil
1 piece (about 4×1 inch) fresh ginger,
    pared and cut into thin strips
1 red bell pepper, cut into thin strips
8 green onions, cut into 1-inch pieces

1. Rinse crabs under cold running water. Gently pull away round hard shell on top. With small sharp knife, gently cut away the gray spongy tissue and discard. Rinse again under cold water.

2. Cut off claws and legs. Pound claws lightly with back of cleaver or hammer to break shells. Chop down center of crab to cut body in half. Cut each half crosswise into 3 pieces.

3. Combine ½ cup of the water, the sherry, sugar, bouillon granules and soy sauce in small bowl; mix well. Blend remaining ¼ cup water and the cornstarch in small cup.

4. Heat vegetable and sesame oils in wok or large skillet over medium heat. Add ginger and stir-fry 1 minute. Add crab pieces; stir-fry 1 minute.

5. Add sherry mixture and red pepper to wok; stir-fry over high heat until liquid boils. Reduce heat; cover and simmer 4 minutes. Stir cornstarch mixture and add to wok. Cook and stir until sauce boils and thickens. Add onions; cook and stir 1 minute more.

Makes 4 to 6 servings

BRAISED TROUT WITH SWEET AND PUNGENT SAUCE

½ cup chicken broth
¼ cup sugar
¼ cup distilled white vinegar
1 tablespoon catsup
1½ teaspoons soy sauce
4 whole cleaned trout (about 8 ounces
    each)
    Salt and pepper
¼ cup plus 2 teaspoons cornstarch,
    divided
3 tablespoons vegetable oil, divided
2 thin slices pared fresh ginger, cut into
    thin shreds
½ small carrot, shredded
¼ cup sliced bamboo shoots (¼ of
    8-ounce can), shredded
¼ cup Chinese mixed pickled vegetables
    (¼ of 12-ounce jar), sliced
2 green onions, cut into 2-inch slivers
1 tablespoon water

1. For sauce, combine chicken broth, sugar, vinegar, catsup and soy sauce in small bowl; mix well.

2. Sprinkle fish lightly with salt and pepper. Lightly coat using ¼ cup of the cornstarch; shake off excess.

3. Heat 2 tablespoons of the oil in large nonstick skillet over medium-high heat. Add fish and cook until lightly browned, about 2 minutes on each side. Remove and set aside.

4. Discard drippings from skillet and wipe clean with paper towels. Heat remaining 1 tablespoon oil in skillet. Add ginger and stir-fry 10 seconds. Add carrot and bamboo shoots; stir-fry 30 seconds. Return fish to wok. Add pickled vegetables and onions. Pour in chicken broth mixture. Cover and simmer until fish turns opaque and flakes easily when tested with fork, about 3 minutes.

5. While fish is cooking, blend remaining 2 teaspoons cornstarch and the water in small cup. Using slotted spoon, transfer fish to serving platter. Pour cornstarch mixture into wok. Cook and stir until sauce boils and thickens. Spoon sauce over fish.

Makes 4 servings

FISH ROLLS WITH CRAB SAUCE

FISH ROLLS

 1 pound sole fillets, ¼- to ⅜-inch thick
   each (about 4 ounces each)
 1 tablespoon dry sherry
 2 teaspoons sesame oil
 1 green onion, minced
 1 teaspoon minced fresh ginger
 ½ teaspoon salt
   Dash ground white pepper

CRAB SAUCE

 1½ tablespoons cornstarch
 2 tablespoons water
 1 tablespoon vegetable oil
 1 teaspoon minced fresh ginger
 2 green onions, thinly sliced
 1 tablespoon dry sherry
 6 ounces fresh crab meat, flaked
 1¼ cups chicken broth
 ¼ cup milk

1. For fish rolls, if fillets are large, cut in half crosswise (each piece should be 5 to 6 inches long). Combine sherry, sesame oil, minced onion, ginger, salt and white pepper in small bowl. Brush each piece of fish with marinade. Let stand 30 minutes.

2. Roll fillets into small bundles. Place on rimmed heatproof dish that will fit inside a steamer. Place dish on rack in steamer. Cover and steam over boiling water until fish turns opaque and flakes easily with fork, 8 to 10 minutes.

3. For crab sauce, blend cornstarch and water in small cup. Heat oil in 2-quart saucepan over medium heat. Add ginger and cook 10 seconds. Add sliced onions, sherry and crab meat; stir-fry 1 minute. Add chicken broth and milk; bring to a simmer. Stir cornstarch mixture and add to saucepan; cook, stirring, until sauce boils and thickens slightly.

4. Using slotted spoon, transfer fish to serving platter. Pour crab sauce over fish.

Makes 4 to 6 servings

BRAISED SHRIMP WITH VEGETABLES

 1 tablespoon vegetable oil
 1 pound large shrimp, shelled and
   deveined
 8 ounces fresh broccoli, cut into small
   pieces
 2 cans (4 ounces each) whole button
   mushrooms, drained
 1 can (8 ounces) bamboo shoots, thinly
   sliced
 ½ cup chicken broth
 1 teaspoon cornstarch
 1 teaspoon oyster sauce
 ¼ teaspoon sugar
 ½ teaspoon minced fresh ginger
 ⅛ teaspoon pepper

1. Heat oil in wok or large skillet over high heat. Add shrimp and stir-fry until shrimp turn pink, about 3 minutes.

2. Add broccoli to wok; stir-fry 1 minute. Add mushrooms and bamboo shoots; stir-fry 1 minute more.

3. Combine remaining ingredients in small bowl; mix well. Pour over shrimp-vegetable mixture. Cook and stir until sauce boils and thickens, about 2 minutes more.

Makes 4 servings

Fish Rolls with Crab Sauce

Seafood Combination

SEAFOOD COMBINATION

Fried Noodles (see page 154)
4 tablespoons vegetable oil, divided
8 green onions, diagonally cut into thin
    slices
3 stalks celery, diagonally cut into thin
    slices
1 can (8 ounces) water chestnuts, drained
    and cut into halves
1 can (8 ounces) bamboo shoots, thinly
    sliced
8 ounces fresh or thawed frozen sea
    scallops, cut into quarters
8 ounces fresh or thawed frozen shrimp,
    shelled and deveined
8 ounces fresh or thawed frozen fish
    fillets, skinned and cut into 1½-inch
    square pieces
8 ounces cleaned, ready-to-cook squid,
    optional
½ cup water
1 tablespoon soy sauce
2 teaspoons dry sherry
2 teaspoons cornstarch
1 teaspoon instant chicken bouillon
    granules

1. Prepare Fried Noodles; set aside.

2. Heat 2 tablespoons of the oil in wok or large skillet over high heat. Add onions, celery, water chestnuts and bamboo shoots; stir-fry until crisp-tender, about 2 minutes. Remove and set aside.

3. Heat remaining 2 tablespoons oil in wok over high heat. Add scallops, shrimp, fish pieces and squid; stir-fry until all fish turns opaque and is cooked through, about 3 minutes.

4. Combine water, soy sauce, sherry, cornstarch and bouillon granules in small bowl. Add to wok. Cook and stir until liquid boils. Return vegetables to wok; cook and stir 2 minutes more. Serve with Fried Noodles. *Makes 6 servings*

BUTTERFLY SHRIMP

1½ pounds large shrimp, shelled and
    deveined, leaving tails intact
3 egg yolks
1½ teaspoons cornstarch
½ teaspoon salt
⅛ teaspoon pepper
2 slices bacon, cut into 1½×¼-inch strips
    Vegetable oil for frying

1. Cut deep slit down back of each shrimp. Flatten cut side slightly with fingers.

2. Beat egg yolks, cornstarch, salt and pepper with fork in medium bowl. Dip each shrimp into egg mixture. Place a bacon strip on cut side of each shrimp.

3. Heat oil in wok or large skillet over medium-high heat to 400°F. Cook shrimp, a few at a time, until golden, 2 to 3 minutes. Drain on paper towels.
Makes 4 to 6 main dish or 8 to 10 appetizer servings

CHINESE STEAMED FISH

1 fresh whole fish (about 2 pounds), such
  as rock cod, red snapper or kingfish;
  or 1 pound fish fillets or steaks, such
  as sea bass, ling cod, halibut or red
  snapper
1 to 2 teaspoons salt
5 green onions
1 piece fresh ginger (about 2 × 1½
  inches), pared and cut into 1½-inch
  slivers
2 tablespoons vegetable oil
2 tablespoons soy sauce
  Cilantro sprigs (Chinese parsley), for
  garnish

1. If using whole fish, clean and scale. Make 3 diagonal slashes on each side. Rub fish with 2 teaspoons salt. (If using fillets, rub with 1 teaspoon salt.) Cut 2 of the green onions into 2-inch pieces. Cut the remaining 3 onions into 1½-inch slivers.

2. Place onion pieces in a rimmed heatproof dish that will fit inside a steamer. Place whole fish on top (or place fillets in single layer on top). Place ½ of ginger and ½ of onion slivers on top of fish.

3. Place dish on rack in steamer. Cover and steam over boiling water until fish turns opaque and flakes easily with fork. Steam about 10 minutes per inch of thickness. While fish is cooking, heat oil in small pan until very hot but not smoking.

4. Remove dish from steamer. Pour off about ½ of pan juices. Pour soy sauce over fish. Sprinkle with remaining ginger and onion slivers. Carefully pour hot oil over fish (oil will sizzle.) Garnish with cilantro sprigs. *Makes 4 to 6 servings*

Chinese Steamed Fish

Clams in Black Bean Sauce

CLAMS IN BLACK BEAN SAUCE

24 small hard-shell clams

1½ tablespoons fermented, salted black beans

2 cloves garlic, minced

1 teaspoon minced fresh ginger

2 tablespoons vegetable oil

2 green onions, thinly sliced

1 cup chicken broth

2 tablespoons dry sherry

1 tablespoon soy sauce

1½ to 2 cups Chinese-style thin egg noodles, cooked and drained

3 tablespoons chopped cilantro (Chinese parsley) or parsley, for garnish

1. Scrub clams under cold running water with stiff brush. (Discard any shells that refuse to close when tapped.)

2. Place black beans in sieve and rinse under cold running water. Coarsely chop beans. Combine beans with garlic and ginger; finely chop all three together.

3. Heat oil in 5-quart pot over medium heat. Add black bean mixture and onions; stir-fry 30 seconds. Add clams and stir to coat.

4. Add chicken broth, sherry and soy sauce to pot. Bring to a boil; reduce heat, cover and simmer until clam shells open, 5 to 8 minutes. (Discard any clams that do not open.)

5. To serve, divide noodles equally among 4 large bowls. Arrange clams on top. Ladle broth over clams. Garnish each serving with chopped cilantro. *Makes 4 servings*

Scallops with Vegetables

SCALLOPS WITH VEGETABLES

1 ounce dried mushrooms
2 tablespoons vegetable oil
2 yellow onions, cut into wedges and
    separated
3 stalks celery, diagonally cut into ½-inch
    pieces
8 ounces fresh green beans, trimmed and
    diagonally cut into 1-inch pieces
2 teaspoons minced fresh ginger
1 clove garlic, minced
1 cup water
2½ tablespoons dry sherry
4 teaspoons soy sauce
4 teaspoons cornstarch
2 teaspoons instant chicken bouillon
    granules
1 pound fresh or thawed frozen sea
    scallops, cut into quarters
6 green onions, diagonally cut into thin
    slices
1 can (15 ounces) baby corn, drained

1. Place mushrooms in bowl and cover with hot water. Let stand 30 minutes. Drain and squeeze out excess water. Cut off and discard stems; cut caps into thin slices.

2. Heat oil in wok or large skillet over high heat. Add yellow onions, celery, green beans, ginger and garlic; stir-fry 3 minutes.

3. Combine water, sherry, soy sauce, cornstarch and bouillon granules in small bowl. Add to wok. Cook and stir until sauce boils.

4. Add scallops, mushrooms, green onions and baby corn. Cook and stir until scallops turn opaque, about 4 minutes.

Makes 4 to 6 servings

SHRIMP OMELETS

3 to 5 tablespoons vegetable oil, divided
8 fresh medium mushrooms, finely
    chopped
1 cup water
4 teaspoons cornstarch
1 teaspoon sugar
2 teaspoons soy sauce
2 teaspoons instant chicken bouillon
    granules
8 eggs
½ teaspoon salt
⅛ teaspoon pepper
8 ounces bean sprouts
8 ounces shrimp, shelled, deveined and
    finely chopped
4 green onions, finely chopped
1 stalk celery, finely chopped
2 green onions, thinly sliced

1. Heat 1 tablespoon of the oil in small skillet. Add mushrooms and cook 1 minute. Remove and set aside.

2. Combine water, cornstarch, sugar, soy sauce and bouillon granules in small saucepan. Cook over medium heat until mixture boils and thickens, about 5 minutes. Keep warm.

3. Combine eggs, salt and pepper in large bowl. Beat until frothy. Add sprouts, shrimp, chopped onions, celery and mushrooms; mix well.

4. For each omelet, heat ½ tablespoon oil in 7-inch omelet pan or skillet. Pour ½ cup egg mixture into pan. Cook until light brown, 2 to 3 minutes on each side. Stack omelets on serving plate. Pour warm soy sauce mixture over omelets. Garnish with sliced onions.

Makes 4 servings

VEGETABLES

CHINESE MIXED PICKLED VEGETABLES

PICKLING LIQUID
- 3 cups sugar
- 3 cups distilled white vinegar
- 1½ cups water
- 1½ teaspoons salt

VEGETABLES
- 3 large carrots, cut into 2-inch long thin strips
- 1 large Chinese white radish (about 1 pound), cut into 2-inch long thin strips
- 1 large cucumber, seeded and cut into 2-inch long thin strips
- 4 stalks celery, diagonally cut into ½-inch pieces
- 8 green onions, diagonally cut into ¼-inch pieces
- 4 ounces fresh ginger, pared and thinly sliced
- 1 large red bell pepper, cut into ½-inch cubes
- 1 large green bell pepper, cut into ½-inch cubes

1. Combine all pickling liquid ingredients in 3-quart saucepan. Bring to a boil, stirring, over medium heat. Cool.

2. For vegetables, fill 5-quart stockpot or Dutch oven ½ full of water. Bring to a boil and add all vegetables. Remove from heat and let stand 2 minutes.

3. Drain vegetables in large colander. Spread vegetables out on clean towels; allow to dry 2 to 3 hours.

4. Pack vegetables firmly into clean jars with tight-fitting lids. Pour Pickling Liquid into jars to cover vegetables. Seal jars tightly. Store in refrigerator at least 1 week before using.

Makes 1½ to 2 quarts

Chinese Mixed Pickled Vegetables

QUICK STIR-FRIED VEGETABLES

2 cups cauliflower florets (about ½ of
   small head)
3 cups broccoli florets (about 1 pound
   broccoli)
½ small jicama (about 8 ounces), pared
2 tablespoons vegetable oil
1 teaspoon minced fresh ginger
½ cup chicken broth, divided
¼ teaspoon salt
¼ teaspoon sugar
1 red bell pepper, cut into thin strips
1 teaspoon sesame oil

1. Cut a small x in stem end of each cauliflower floret. If florets are large, cut them into 2 or 3 slices. Cut a small x in stem end of broccoli florets. Cut jicama into thick slices, then cut into 2×¼-inch strips. Set all vegetables, oil and seasonings near cooking area.

2. Heat vegetable oil in wok or large skillet over high heat. Add ginger and stir-fry 10 seconds. Add cauliflower and broccoli; stir-fry 30 seconds to coat with oil.

3. Pour about ⅓ cup of the chicken broth around edges of wok. Add salt and sugar. Cover and cook until vegetables are partially tender, 3 to 4 minutes.

4. Add jicama, bell pepper and remaining chicken broth. Cover and cook 1 minute. Uncover and stir-fry until vegetables are crisp-tender and all liquid has evaporated. Stir in sesame oil.

Makes 4 to 6 servings

Quick Stir-Fried Vegetables

SHRIMP-STUFFED BEAN CURD

SHRIMP STUFFING

- 4 ounces shrimp, shelled, deveined and finely chopped
- 2 tablespoons minced water chestnuts
- 2 teaspoons minced green onions
- 1 teaspoon dry sherry
- 1 teaspoon cornstarch
- ¼ teaspoon salt
- ½ teaspoon sesame oil

BEAN CURD

- 1 package (about 1 pound) bean curd
- 3 tablespoons vegetable oil, divided
- 1 cup chicken broth
- 1 tablespoon soy sauce
- ½ teaspoon sugar
- ½ teaspoon fresh ginger
- ½ small head napa cabbage, cut into 2-inch squares
- ½ cup straw mushrooms
- ¼ cup thawed frozen peas
- 1 tablespoon cornstarch
- 1 tablespoon water

1. Combine all shrimp stuffing ingredients in medium bowl; mix well.

2. Drain bean curd. Cut bean curd crosswise through the middle to make 8 triangles. Place between paper towels and gently press out excess water.

3. Cut a pocket in longest side of each triangle. Scoop out ½-inch hole with spoon or knife. Fill hole with 1 tablespoon shrimp filling. Smooth top.

4. Heat 2 tablespoons of the oil in wok or large nonstick skillet over medium heat. Add stuffed bean curd triangles, flat-side down. Cook until golden brown, about 3 minutes on each side. Stand triangles in wok and cook filled-side down 30 seconds. Remove and set aside. Discard drippings; wipe wok clean with paper towels.

5. Combine chicken broth, soy sauce and sugar in small bowl. Heat remaining 1 tablespoon oil in wok over medium-high heat. Add ginger and stir-fry 10 seconds. Add cabbage; stir-fry until cabbage begins to wilt, about 2 minutes. Arrange bean curd triangles on top of cabbage. Sprinkle with straw mushrooms and peas.

6. Pour chicken broth mixture over bean curd. Cover and bring just to a boil; reduce heat and simmer 10 minutes. Blend cornstarch and water in small cup. Gently push bean curd to one side of wok; stir cornstarch mixture into liquid. Cook, stirring carefully, until sauce boils and thickens. *Makes 4 servings*

Ma-Po Bean Curd

CHINESE VEGETABLES

1 pound fresh broccoli
¾ cup water
1 tablespoon instant chicken bouillon
    granules
2 tablespoons vegetable oil
2 medium yellow onions, cut into wedges
    and separated
1 tablespoon minced fresh ginger
8 ounces fresh spinach, coarsely chopped
8 ounces fresh snow peas or 1 package
    (6 ounces) thawed frozen snow peas,
    trimmed and strings removed
4 stalks celery, diagonally cut into ½-inch
    pieces
8 green onions, diagonally cut into thin
    slices

1. Cut broccoli tops into florets. Cut stalks into 2×¼-inch thin strips. Combine water and bouillon granules in small bowl; mix well.

2. Heat oil in wok or large skillet over high heat. Add broccoli stalks, yellow onions and ginger; stir-fry 1 minute. Add all remaining vegetables; toss lightly.

3. Add water mixture. Toss until vegetables are well coated. Bring to a boil, cover and cook until vegetables are crisp-tender, 2 to 3 minutes. *Makes 4 to 6 servings*

NOTE: Sliced carrots, zucchini, green beans or green bell peppers may be used in addition to, or in place of, the listed vegetables.

MA–PO BEAN CURD

1 tablespoon Szechuan peppercorns,
    optional
¾ cup chicken broth
1 tablespoon soy sauce
1 tablespoon dry sherry
2 tablespoons vegetable oil
4 ounces ground pork
2 teaspoons minced fresh ginger
2 cloves garlic, minced
1 tablespoon hot bean sauce
12 to 14 ounces bean curd, drained and cut
    into ½-inch cubes
2 green onions, thinly sliced
3 tablespoons water
1½ tablespoons cornstarch
1 teaspoon sesame oil

1. Place peppercorns in small dry skillet; shake over medium-low heat, until fragrant, about 2 minutes. Let cool. Crush peppercorns with mortar and pestle or place between paper towels and crush with hammer.*

2. Combine chicken broth, soy sauce and sherry in small bowl.

3. Heat vegetable oil in wok or large skillet over high heat. Add pork and stir-fry until pork is no longer pink, about 2 minutes. Add ginger, garlic and hot bean sauce. Stir-fry until meat absorbs color from bean sauce, about 1 minute.

4. Add chicken broth mixture and bean curd to wok. Simmer, uncovered, 5 minutes. Stir in onions. Blend water and cornstarch in small cup. Add to wok; cook and stir until sauce boils and thickens slightly. Stir in sesame oil. Pass ground peppercorns separately to sprinkle over each serving, if desired.
Makes 3 to 4 servings

*Note: Szechuan peppercorns are deceptively potent. Wear rubber or plastic gloves when crushing them and do not touch eyes or lips when handling.

ZUCCHINI SHANGHAI STYLE

4 dried mushrooms
½ cup chicken broth
2 tablespoons catsup
2 teaspoons soy sauce
1 teaspoon dry sherry
¼ teaspoon sugar
⅛ teaspoon salt
1 teaspoon red wine vinegar
2 tablespoons vegetable oil, divided
1 teaspoon minced fresh ginger
1 clove garlic, minced
1 green onion, minced
1 large tomato, peeled, seeded and
    chopped
4 tablespoons water, divided
1 teaspoon cornstarch
1 pound zucchini, diagonally cut into
    1-inch pieces
½ small yellow onion, cut into wedges and
    separated

1. Place mushrooms in bowl and cover with hot water. Let stand 30 minutes. Drain, reserving ¼ cup liquid. Squeeze out excess water. Cut off and discard stems; cut caps into thin slices.

2. Combine the reserved ¼ cup mushroom liquid, the chicken broth, catsup, soy sauce, sherry, sugar, salt and vinegar in small bowl.

3. Heat 1 tablespoon of the oil in 2-quart saucepan over medium-high heat. Add ginger and garlic and stir-fry 10 seconds. Add mushrooms, green onion and tomato. Stir-fry 1 minute. Add chicken broth mixture and bring to a boil; reduce heat and simmer, uncovered, 10 minutes.

4. Blend 1 tablespoon of the water and the cornstarch in small cup. Heat remaining 1 tablespoon oil in wok or large skillet over medium-high heat. Add zucchini and yellow onion and stir-fry 30 seconds. Add remaining 2 tablespoons water, cover and cook, stirring occasionally, until vegetables are crisp-tender, 3 to 4 minutes.

5. Pour tomato sauce into wok. Stir cornstarch mixture and add to wok. Cook and stir until sauce boils and thickens.

Makes 4 to 6 servings

BEAN CURD WITH OYSTER SAUCE

2 tablespoons vegetable oil, divided
8 ounces bean curd, cut into ½-inch cubes
½ cup water
2 tablespoons oyster sauce
1 tablespoon cornstarch
4 teaspoons dry sherry
4 teaspoons soy sauce
4 ounces fresh mushrooms, sliced
6 green onions, cut into 1-inch pieces
3 stalks celery, diagonally cut into ½-inch
    pieces
1 red or green bell pepper, cut into ½-inch
    chunks

1. Heat 1 tablespoon of the oil in wok or large skillet over high heat. Add bean curd and stir-fry until light brown, about 3 minutes. Remove and set aside. Combine water, oyster sauce, cornstarch, sherry and soy sauce in small bowl.

2. Heat remaining 1 tablespoon oil in wok over high heat. Add all vegetables; stir-fry 1 minute.

3. Return bean curd to wok; toss lightly to combine. Add cornstarch-soy mixture to wok. Cook and stir until liquid boils; cook 1 minute more.

Makes 4 servings

Zucchini Shanghai Style

BRAISED CHOICE VEGETABLES

8 dried mushrooms
1 can (15 ounces) peeled straw
   mushrooms
1 cup baby corn (½ of 15-ounce can)
½ cup sliced bamboo shoots (½ of
   8-ounce can)
2 tablespoons oyster sauce
2 teaspoons soy sauce
2 tablespoons vegetable oil
1 clove garlic, minced
½ cup chicken broth
2 teaspoons cornstarch
1 tablespoon water

1. Place dried mushrooms in bowl and cover with hot water. Let stand 30 minutes. Drain, reserving ½ cup liquid. Squeeze out excess water. Cut off and discard stems. Leave mushrooms whole, or, if large, cut into halves.

2. Drain straw mushrooms, baby corn and bamboo shoots. If corn is large, diagonally cut each ear into small pieces. Rinse under cold running water and drain. Combine oyster sauce and soy sauce in small cup.

3. Heat oil in wok or large skillet over high heat. Add garlic and stir-fry 10 seconds. Add dried mushrooms; stir-fry 1 minute. Add chicken broth and reserved ½ cup mushroom liquid. Cover and simmer over medium heat until mushrooms are tender and about ½ the liquid has evaporated, about 5 minutes.

4. Add straw mushrooms, corn, bamboo shoots and soy sauce mixture. Simmer 3 minutes. Blend cornstarch and water in small cup. Stir into wok; cook and stir until sauce boils and thickens slightly. *Makes 4 to 6 servings*

RICE & NOODLES

FRIED RICE

3 cups water
1½ teaspoons salt
1½ cups long-grain rice
4 slices bacon, chopped
3 eggs
⅛ teaspoon pepper
3 tablespoons vegetable oil, divided
2 teaspoons minced fresh ginger
8 ounces Barbecued Pork (see page 88),
    cut into thin strips
8 ounces cooked shrimp, shelled,
    deveined and coarsely chopped
8 green onions, finely chopped
1 to 2 tablespoons soy sauce

1. Combine water and salt in 3-quart saucepan. Cover and bring to a boil. Stir in rice; reduce heat. Cover and simmer until rice is tender, 15 to 20 minutes; drain.

2. Cook bacon in wok over medium heat, stirring often, until crisp; drain. Remove all but 1 tablespoon bacon drippings from wok.

3. Beat eggs and pepper with fork in small bowl. Pour ⅓ of egg mixture into wok. Tilt wok slightly so egg covers bottom. Cook over medium heat until eggs are set, 1 to 2 minutes. Remove from wok. Roll up omelet and cut into thin strips. Pour ½ tablespoon of the oil into wok. Add ½ of remaining egg mixture; tilt wok and cook until eggs are set. Remove, roll up and cut into thin strips. Repeat with another ½ tablespoon oil and remaining eggs.

4. Heat remaining 2 tablespoons oil in wok over medium-high heat. Add ginger and stir-fry 1 minute. Add rice; cook and stir 5 minutes. Stir in eggs, bacon, pork, shrimp, onions and soy sauce. Cook and stir until heated through. *Makes 6 to 8 servings*

VERMICELLI

8 ounces Chinese rice vermicelli or bean
    threads
Vegetable oil for frying

1. Cut bundle of vermicelli in half. Gently pull each half apart into small bunches.

2. Heat oil in wok or large skillet over medium-high heat to 375°F. Using tongs or slotted spoon, lower a small bunch of vermicelli into hot oil. Cook until vermicelli rises to top, 3 to 5 seconds. Immediately remove and drain on paper towels. Repeat with remaining bunches. *Makes about 4 servings*

Fried Rice

Lo Mein Noodles with Shrimp

LO MEIN NOODLES WITH SHRIMP

12 ounces Chinese-style thin egg noodles
2 teaspoons sesame oil
1½ tablespoons oyster sauce
1½ tablespoons soy sauce
½ teaspoon sugar
¼ teaspoon salt
¼ teaspoon ground white pepper
2 tablespoons vegetable oil
1 teaspoon minced fresh ginger
1 clove garlic, minced
8 ounces medium shrimp, shelled and
    deveined
1 tablespoon dry sherry
½ cup Chinese chives, cut into 1-inch
    pieces or ¼ cup domestic chives, cut
    into 1-inch pieces and 2 green onions,
    cut into 1-inch pieces
8 ounces bean sprouts

1. Cook noodles according to package directions until tender but still firm, 2 to 3 minutes. Drain, rinse under cold running water and drain again. Toss noodles with sesame oil until well coated.

2. Combine oyster sauce, soy sauce, sugar, salt and pepper in small bowl.

3. Heat vegetable oil in wok or large skillet over high heat. Add ginger and garlic and stir-fry 10 seconds. Add shrimp; stir-fry until shrimp begin to turn pink, about 1 minute. Add sherry and chives; stir-fry until chives begin to wilt, about 15 seconds. Add ½ of bean sprouts; stir-fry 15 seconds. Add remaining bean sprouts; stir-fry 15 seconds more.

4. Add oyster sauce mixture and noodles. Cook and stir until heated through, about 2 minutes. *Makes 4 servings*

STEAMED RICE

1 cup long-grain rice
2 cups water
1 teaspoon salt
1 tablespoon vegetable oil

1. Place rice in strainer and rinse under cold running water to remove excess starch. Combine rice, water, salt and oil in 3-quart saucepan.

2. Cook over medium-high heat until water boils. Reduce heat to low, cover and simmer until rice is tender, 15 to 20 minutes.

3. Remove from heat; let stand 5 minutes. Uncover and fluff rice lightly with fork.   *Makes 3 cups*

NOODLE BASKETS

8 ounces Chinese-style thin egg noodles
  Vegetable oil for frying

1. Cook noodles according to package directions until tender but still firm, 2 to 3 minutes. Drain, rinse under cold running water and drain again.

2. Place several layers of paper towels over cookie sheets or jelly-roll pans. Spread noodles over paper towels and let dry at least 8 hours or overnight.

3. Brush inside of medium strainer (about 5 inches in diameter) with a small amount of oil. Spread an even layer of noodles about ½ inch thick in strainer. Brush rounded outside of another strainer with oil. Place second strainer rounded-side down over noodles in first strainer. Press lightly.

4. Heat remaining oil in wok or deep saucepan over medium-high heat to 375°F. Carefully lower the two strainers, holding handles together, into hot oil. Cook until noodles are golden, 2 to 3 minutes. Remove from oil and place on paper towels. Carefully remove top and bottom strainers, running knife blade around edge of noodles if necessary to loosen noodle basket. Drain baskets on paper towels. Repeat with remaining noodles.

Makes 6 to 8 baskets

Note: These noodle baskets can be used to serve Chinese food in an unusual and attractive way. To prepare in advance, cook as directed, wrap securely in plastic wrap and store in refrigerator up to three days or in freezer up to three weeks. To reheat, remove from plastic, arrange on cookie sheet, and bake in preheated 325°F oven until heated through, 8 to 10 minutes.

NOODLES WITH SIMMERED CHICKEN

4 dried mushrooms
2 teaspoons dry sherry
1 boneless, skinless chicken breast half,
  thinly sliced
1 small bunch watercress or ½ bunch
  fresh spinach leaves
8 ounces Chinese-style thin egg noodles
2 cups chicken broth
1 tablespoon soy sauce
¼ cup sliced bamboo shoots
1 teaspoon sesame oil
  Dash ground white pepper
2 green onions, thinly sliced

1. Place mushrooms in bowl and cover with hot water. Let stand 30 minutes. Drain and squeeze out excess water. Cut off and discard stems; cut caps into thin slices.

2. Sprinkle sherry over chicken slices in medium bowl; let stand 15 minutes.

3. Wash watercress and discard thick stems. If using spinach, wash and remove stems; cut into 2-inch wide strips.

4. Cook noodles according to package directions until tender but still firm, 2 to 3 minutes. Drain, rinse under cold running water and drain again.

5. Bring chicken broth and soy sauce to a boil in 3-quart saucepan. Add mushrooms, chicken and bamboo shoots. Reduce heat and simmer, uncovered, about 4 minutes. Add watercress, sesame oil and pepper; simmer 1 minute. Add noodles and cook until heated through.

6. Divide noodles, chicken and vegetables between 2 serving bowls. Ladle broth over noodles. Sprinkle each serving with onions.   *Makes 2 servings*

COLD STIRRED NOODLES

DRESSING
  6 tablespoons soy sauce
  2 tablespoons sesame oil
  ¼ cup red wine vinegar
2½ tablespoons sugar
  ¼ to ½ teaspoon chili oil (or to taste)

NOODLES
  1 pound Chinese-style thin egg noodles
  1 tablespoon sesame oil
  2 small carrots, cut into 3-inch pieces and
    shredded
  3 cups bean sprouts
  ½ large thin-skinned cucumber, cut into
    3-inch pieces and shredded
  1 bunch radishes, shredded
  4 green onions, cut into 2-inch slivers
  1 cup matchstick strips
    Barbecued Pork (see page 88), optional

1. Combine all dressing ingredients in small bowl; mix well.

2. Cut noodles into 6-inch pieces. Cook noodles according to package directions until tender but still firm, 2 to 3 minutes. Drain, rinse under cold running water and drain again. Toss noodles with sesame oil until well coated. Refrigerate until ready to serve.

3. Cook carrots in pot of boiling water 30 seconds; drain and rinse under cold running water. Cook bean sprouts in boiling water 30 seconds; drain and rinse under cold running water.

4. To serve, arrange noodles on large platter. Arrange all remaining vegetables and pork on top; sprinkle with onions. Pass dressing separately.   *Makes 6 to 8 servings*

BEAN THREADS WITH MINCED PORK

4 ounces bean threads or Chinese rice
    vermicelli
3 dried mushrooms
1 small red or green hot chili pepper
3 green onions
2 tablespoons minced fresh ginger
2 tablespoons hot bean sauce
1½ cups chicken broth
1 tablespoon soy sauce
1 tablespoon dry sherry
2 tablespoons vegetable oil
6 ounces lean ground pork
2 cilantro sprigs (Chinese parsley), for
    garnish

1. Place bean threads and dried mushrooms in separate bowls. Cover each with hot water. Let stand 30 minutes; drain. Cut bean threads into 4-inch pieces. Squeeze out excess water from mushrooms. Cut off and discard stems; cut caps into thin slices.

2. Cut chili pepper in half and scrape out seeds.* Finely mince chili pepper. Thinly slice 2 of the green onions. Cut remaining onion into 1½-inch slivers and reserve for garnish. Combine ginger and hot bean sauce in small bowl. Combine chicken broth, soy sauce and sherry in medium bowl.

3. Heat oil in wok or large skillet over high heat. Add pork and stir-fry until meat is no longer pink, about 2 minutes. Add chili pepper, sliced onions and ginger-bean sauce mixture. Stir-fry until meat absorbs color from bean sauce, about 1 minute.

4. Add chicken broth mixture, bean threads and mushrooms. Simmer, uncovered, until most of the liquid is absorbed, about 5 minutes. Garnish with onion slivers and cilantro sprigs.

Makes 4 servings

*Note: Wear rubber or plastic gloves when cutting chili peppers. Do not touch eyes or lips when handling.

FRIED NOODLES

8 ounces Chinese-style thin egg noodles
Salt
Vegetable oil for frying

1. Cook noodles according to package directions until tender but still firm, 2 to 3 minutes. Drain, rinse under cold running water and drain again.

2. Place several layers of paper towels over cookie sheets or jelly-roll pans. Spread noodles over paper towels and let dry 2 to 3 hours.

3. Heat oil in wok or large skillet over medium-high heat to 375°F. Using tongs or slotted spoon, lower a small portion of noodles into hot oil. Cook until golden, about 30 seconds. Drain on paper towels. Repeat with remaining noodles.

Makes 4 servings

Vegetarian Fried Rice

VEGETARIAN FRIED RICE

4 dried mushrooms
4 cups cooked long-grain rice
3 eggs
¾ teaspoon salt, divided
2½ tablespoons vegetable oil, divided
1 teaspoon minced fresh ginger
1 clove garlic, minced
3 green onions, thinly sliced
4 ounces bean curd, cut into ¼-inch cubes
    and deep fried
1 tablespoon soy sauce
¼ teaspoon sugar
1 cup bean sprouts, coarsely chopped
½ cup thawed frozen peas

1. Place mushrooms in small bowl and cover with hot water. Let stand 30 minutes. Drain, reserving liquid. Squeeze out excess water. Cut off and discard stems; dice caps.

2. Rub rice with wet hands so all the grains are separated.

3. Beat eggs with ¼ teaspoon of the salt in medium bowl. Heat ½ tablespoon oil in wok or large skillet over medium heat. Add eggs; cook and stir until soft curds form. Remove from heat and cut eggs into small pieces using a spoon. Remove and set aside.

4. Heat remaining 2 tablespoons oil in wok over high heat. Add ginger, garlic and onions; stir-fry 10 seconds. Add mushrooms, ¼ cup of the reserved mushroom soaking liquid, the bean curd, soy sauce and sugar. Cook until most of the liquid evaporates, about 4 minutes. Add bean sprouts and peas; cook 30 seconds.

5. Add rice and remaining ½ teaspoon salt. Stir and toss until heated through. Add a few drops mushroom soaking liquid if rice appears dry. Fold in eggs before serving. *Makes 4 servings*

Spicy Beef With Noodles (page 170)

Light & Easy Chinese

APPETIZERS & SOUPS

BEEF SOUP WITH NOODLES

2 tablespoons soy sauce
1 teaspoon minced fresh ginger
¼ teaspoon crushed red pepper flakes
1 boneless beef top sirloin steak, cut
    1 inch thick (about ¾ pound)
1 tablespoon peanut or vegetable oil
2 cups sliced fresh mushrooms
2 cans (about 14 ounces each) beef broth
3 ounces (1 cup) fresh snow peas, cut
    diagonally into 1-inch pieces
1½ cups hot cooked fine egg noodles
    (2 ounces uncooked)
1 green onion, cut diagonally into thin
    slices
1 teaspoon Oriental sesame oil (optional)
    Red bell pepper strips for garnish
    Easy Wonton Chips (page 164)

1. Combine soy sauce, ginger and crushed red pepper in small bowl. Spread mixture evenly over both sides of steak. Marinate at room temperature 15 minutes.

2. Heat deep skillet over medium-high heat. Add peanut oil; heat until hot. Drain steak; reserve soy sauce mixture (there will only be a small amount of mixture). Add steak to skillet; cook 4 to 5 minutes per side.* Let stand on cutting board 10 minutes.

3. Add mushrooms to skillet; stir-fry 2 minutes. Add broth, snow peas and reserved soy sauce mixture; bring to a boil, scraping up browned meat bits. Reduce heat to medium-low. Stir in noodles.

4. Cut steak across the grain into ⅛-inch slices; cut each slice into 1-inch pieces. Stir into soup; heat through. Stir in onion and sesame oil. Ladle into soup bowls. Garnish with red pepper strips.

Makes 4 main-dish or 6 appetizer servings (about 6 cups)

*Cooking time is for medium-rare doneness. Adjust time for desired doneness.

CHILLED SHRIMP IN CHINESE MUSTARD SAUCE

1 cup water
½ cup dry white wine
2 tablespoons soy sauce
½ teaspoon Szechuan or black
    peppercorns
1 pound large raw shrimp, peeled,
    deveined
¼ cup sweet and sour sauce
2 teaspoons Chinese hot mustard

1. Combine water, wine, soy sauce and peppercorns in medium saucepan. Bring to a boil over high heat. Add shrimp; reduce heat to medium. Cover and simmer 2 to 3 minutes until shrimp are opaque. Drain well. Cover and refrigerate until chilled.

2. Combine sweet and sour sauce and hot mustard in small bowl; mix well. Serve as a dipping sauce for shrimp.

Makes 6 appetizer servings

*Clockwise from top right: Wonton Soup, Easy
Wonton Chips, Beef Soup with Noodles*

Shrimp Toast

SHRIMP TOAST

½ pound raw shrimp, peeled, deveined
2 tablespoons chopped green onion
2 tablespoons finely chopped water chestnuts
2 tablespoons soy sauce
1 teaspoon Oriental sesame oil
1 egg white, slightly beaten
6 slices white sandwich bread, crusts removed
   Red and yellow bell peppers for garnish

1. Finely chop shrimp. If using food processor, process with on/off pulses, about 10 times or until shrimp are finely chopped.

2. Combine shrimp, onion, water chestnuts, soy sauce and sesame oil in medium bowl; mix well. Stir in egg white; mix well.*

3. Toast bread lightly on both sides. Cut toast diagonally into quarters. Spread shrimp mixture evenly over toast to edges.

4. Place toast on foil-lined baking sheet or broiler pan. Broil 6 inches from heat 4 minutes or until lightly browned. Garnish with peppers. *Makes 2 dozen appetizers*

Note: For information on storing unused water chestnuts, see page 7.

*The filling may be made ahead to this point; cover and refrigerate filling up to 24 hours. Proceed as directed in step 3.

SHANTUNG TWIN MUSHROOM SOUP

1 package (1 ounce) dried black Chinese mushrooms*
1 tablespoon peanut or vegetable oil
1 large onion, coarsely chopped
2 cloves garlic, minced
2 cups sliced fresh mushrooms
2 cans (about 14 ounces each) chicken broth
2 ounces cooked ham, cut into thin slivers (½ cup)
½ cup thinly sliced green onions
1 tablespoon soy sauce
1 tablespoon dry sherry
1 tablespoon cornstarch

1. Place dried mushrooms in small bowl; cover with warm water. Soak 30 minutes to soften. Drain; squeeze out excess water. Discard stems; slice caps.

2. Heat large saucepan over medium heat. Add oil; heat until hot. Add chopped onion and garlic; cook 1 minute. Add dried and fresh mushrooms; cook 4 minutes, stirring occasionally.

3. Add broth; bring to a boil over high heat. Reduce heat to medium-low. Cover and simmer 15 minutes.

4. Stir in ham and green onions; heat through. Blend soy sauce and sherry into cornstarch in cup until smooth. Stir into soup. Cook 2 minutes or until soup thickens, stirring occasionally. Ladle into soup bowls.
Makes 6 appetizer servings (about 5½ cups)

*Or, substitute 4 ounces fresh shiitake mushrooms; discard stems and slice caps. Omit step 1.

ORIENTAL CHICKEN WINGS

12 chicken wings *or* 24 chicken drumettes
¼ cup *plus* 2 teaspoons soy sauce, divided
2 tablespoons dry sherry
2 cloves garlic, minced
2 teaspoons brown sugar
½ cup lite or fat-free mayonnaise
1 teaspoon rice vinegar
½ teaspoon Oriental sesame oil

1. Cut off chicken wing tips at joint; discard tips or save for making chicken broth. Cut each remaining wing portion at other joint to make 2 pieces. Place in large plastic bag.

2. Combine ¼ cup soy sauce, sherry, garlic and brown sugar in cup; pour over chicken wings. Close bag securely; turn to coat. Marinate in refrigerator at least 4 hours or up to 24 hours.

3. Combine mayonnaise, vinegar, sesame oil and remaining 2 teaspoons soy sauce in small bowl. Cover and refrigerate until ready to serve.

4. Drain chicken wings; reserve marinade. Place wings on rack of broiler pan. Brush with half of reserved marinade. Broil 6 inches from heat 10 minutes. Turn wings over; brush with remaining marinade. Broil 10 minutes or until chicken is browned and cooked through. Serve mayonnaise mixture as a dipping sauce for wings. *Makes 2 dozen appetizers*

CRAB CAKES CANTON

½ pound thawed frozen cooked crabmeat
    or imitation crabmeat, drained and
    flaked or finely chopped (about
    2 cups)
1½ cups fresh bread crumbs
¼ cup thinly sliced green onions
1 clove garlic, minced
1 teaspoon minced fresh ginger
2 egg whites, slightly beaten
3 tablespoons oyster sauce
4 teaspoons peanut or vegetable oil,
    divided
    Sweet and sour sauce

1. Combine crabmeat, bread crumbs, onions, garlic and ginger in medium bowl; mix well. Add egg whites and oyster sauce; mix well.

2. Shape into 12 patties, about ½ inch thick and 2 inches in diameter.* Heat large nonstick skillet over medium heat. Add 2 teaspoons oil; heat until hot.

3. Cook 6 crab cakes in hot oil 2 minutes per side or until golden brown. Remove to warm serving plate; keep warm. Repeat with remaining oil and crab cakes. Serve with sweet and sour sauce. *Makes 12 appetizers*

Note: To reheat cooked crab cakes, place in single layer on baking sheet. Bake in preheated 350°F oven 9 to 10 minutes until heated through.

*Crab mixture may be made ahead to this point; cover and refrigerate up to 24 hours before cooking. Proceed as directed in step 2.

Marinated Beef Skewers

MINI–MARINATED BEEF SKEWERS

1 boneless beef sirloin steak, cut 1 inch
    thick (about 1 pound)
2 tablespoons soy sauce
2 tablespoons dry sherry
1 tablespoon Oriental sesame oil
2 cloves garlic, minced
18 cherry tomatoes
    Lettuce leaves (optional)

1. Cut beef across the grain into ⅛-inch slices. Place in large plastic bag. Combine soy sauce, sherry, sesame oil and garlic in cup; pour over steak. Close bag securely; turn to coat. Marinate in refrigerator at least 30 minutes or up to 2 hours.

2. Soak 18 (6-inch) wooden skewers in water to cover 20 minutes.

3. Drain steak; discard marinade. Weave beef accordion-fashion onto skewers. Place on rack of broiler pan.

4. Broil 4 to 5 inches from heat 2 minutes. Turn skewers over; broil 2 minutes or until beef is barely pink in center.

5. Garnish each skewer with one cherry tomato; place on lettuce-lined platter. Serve warm or at room temperature.

Makes 18 appetizers

WONTON SOUP

¼ pound ground pork, chicken or turkey
¼ cup finely chopped water chestnuts
2 tablespoons soy sauce, divided
1 teaspoon minced fresh ginger
1 egg white, slightly beaten
12 wonton wrappers
1 can (46 ounces) chicken broth
1½ cups sliced fresh spinach leaves
1 cup thinly sliced cooked pork (optional)
½ cup diagonally sliced green onions
1 tablespoon Oriental sesame oil
   Shredded carrot for garnish

1. Combine ground pork, water chestnuts, 1 tablespoon soy sauce, ginger and egg white in small bowl; mix well.

2. Place 1 wonton wrapper with a point toward edge of counter. Mound 1 teaspoon of filling toward bottom point. Fold bottom point over filling, then roll wrapper over once. Moisten inside points with water. Bring side points together below the filling, overlapping slightly; press together firmly to seal. Repeat with remaining wrappers and filling.* Keep finished wontons covered with plastic wrap, while filling remaining wrappers.

3. Combine broth and remaining 1 tablespoon soy sauce in large saucepan. Bring to a boil over high heat. Reduce heat to medium; add wontons. Simmer, uncovered, 4 minutes.

4. Stir in spinach, cooked pork and onions; remove from heat. Stir in sesame oil. Ladle into soup bowls. Garnish with shredded carrot.   *Makes 4 to 6 appetizer servings (about 7 cups)*

Note: For information on storing unused water chestnuts, see page 7.

*Wontons may be made ahead to this point; cover and refrigerate up to 8 hours or freeze up to 3 months. Proceed as directed in step 3, if using refrigerated wontons. Increase simmer time to 6 minutes, if using frozen wontons.

EASY WONTON CHIPS

1 tablespoon soy sauce
2 teaspoons peanut or vegetable oil
½ teaspoon sugar
¼ teaspoon garlic salt
12 wonton wrappers

1. Preheat oven to 375°F.

2. Combine soy sauce, oil, sugar and garlic salt in small bowl; mix well.

3. Cut each wonton wrapper diagonally in half. Place wonton wrappers on 15×10-inch jelly-roll pan coated with nonstick cooking spray. Brush soy sauce mixture lightly but evenly over both sides of each wonton wrapper.

4. Bake 4 to 6 minutes or until crisp and lightly browned, turning after 3 minutes. Transfer to cooling rack; cool completely.
        Makes 2 dozen chips

CHINATOWN STUFFED MUSHROOMS

24 large fresh mushrooms (about 1 pound)
½ pound ground pork or turkey
1 clove garlic, minced
¼ cup fine dry bread crumbs
¼ cup thinly sliced green onions
3 tablespoons soy sauce, divided
1 teaspoon minced fresh ginger
1 egg white, slightly beaten
⅛ teaspoon crushed red pepper flakes
    (optional)

1. Remove stems from mushrooms; finely chop enough stems to equal 1 cup. Reserve remaining stems for use in salads, soups or stews, if desired. Cook pork with chopped stems and garlic in medium skillet over medium-high heat until pork is no longer pink, stirring to separate pork. Spoon off fat.

2. Stir in bread crumbs, onions, 2 tablespoons soy sauce, ginger, egg white and crushed red pepper; mix well.

3. Brush mushrooms lightly on all sides with remaining 1 tablespoon soy sauce; spoon about 2 teaspoons stuffing into each mushroom cap.* Place stuffed mushrooms on rack of foil-lined broiler pan. Broil 4 to 5 inches from heat 5 to 6 minutes until hot. *Makes 2 dozen appetizers*

*Mushrooms may be made ahead to this point; cover and refrigerate up to 24 hours. Increase broiling time by 1 to 2 minutes for the chilled mushrooms.

SPICY BEEF TURNOVERS

½ pound lean ground beef or turkey
2 cloves garlic, minced
2 tablespoons soy sauce
1 tablespoon water
½ teaspoon cornstarch
1 teaspoon curry powder
¼ teaspoon Chinese five-spice powder
¼ teaspoon crushed red pepper flakes
2 tablespoons minced green onion
1 package (7.5 ounces) refrigerated
    biscuits
1 egg
1 tablespoon water

1. Preheat oven to 400°F. Cook beef with garlic in medium skillet over medium-high heat until beef is no longer pink, stirring to separate beef. Spoon off fat.

2. Blend soy sauce and water into cornstarch in cup until smooth. Add soy sauce mixture along with curry powder, five-spice powder and crushed red pepper to skillet. Cook and stir 30 seconds or until liquid is absorbed, stirring constantly. Remove from heat; stir in onion.

3. Roll each biscuit between 2 sheets of waxed paper into 4-inch rounds. Spoon heaping 1 tablespoon beef mixture onto one side of each biscuit; fold over, forming a semi-circle. Pinch edges together to seal.

4. Arrange turnovers on baking sheet coated with nonstick cooking spray. Beat egg with water in cup; brush lightly over turnovers. Bake 9 to 10 minutes until golden brown. Serve warm or at room temperature. *Makes 10 appetizers*

SPICY CHICKEN BUNDLES

1 pound ground chicken or turkey
2 teaspoons minced fresh ginger
2 cloves garlic, minced
¼ teaspoon crushed red pepper flakes
3 tablespoons soy sauce
1 tablespoon cornstarch
1 tablespoon peanut or vegetable oil
⅓ cup finely chopped water chestnuts
⅓ cup thinly sliced green onions
¼ cup chopped peanuts
12 large lettuce leaves, such as romaine
  Chinese hot mustard (optional)

1. Combine chicken, ginger, garlic and crushed red pepper in medium bowl.

2. Blend soy sauce into cornstarch in cup until smooth.

3. Heat wok or large skillet over medium-high heat. Add oil; heat until hot. Add chicken mixture; stir-fry 2 to 3 minutes until chicken is no longer pink.

4. Stir soy sauce mixture and add to wok. Stir-fry 30 seconds or until sauce boils and thickens. Add water chestnuts, onions and peanuts; heat through.*

5. Divide filling evenly among lettuce leaves; roll up. Secure with wooden toothpicks. Serve warm or at room temperature. Do not let filling stand at room temperature more than 2 hours. Serve with hot mustard.   *Makes 12 appetizers*

Note: For information on storing unused water chestnuts, see page 7.

*Filling may be made ahead to this point; cover and refrigerate up to 4 hours. Just before rolling in lettuce, reheat chicken filling until warm. Proceed as directed in step 5.

SPRING ROLLS

1 cup preshredded cabbage or coleslaw
  mix
½ cup finely chopped cooked ham
¼ cup finely chopped water chestnuts
¼ cup thinly sliced green onions
3 tablespoons plum sauce, divided
1 teaspoon Oriental sesame oil
3 flour tortillas (6 to 7 inches)

1. Combine cabbage, ham, water chestnuts, onions, 2 tablespoons plum sauce and sesame oil in medium bowl; mix well.

2. Spread remaining 1 tablespoon plum sauce evenly over tortillas. Spread about ½ cup cabbage mixture on each tortilla to within ¼ inch of edge; roll up.

3. Wrap each tortilla tightly in plastic wrap. Refrigerate at least 1 hour or up to 24 hours before serving.

4. Cut each tortilla diagonally into 4 pieces.

Makes 12 appetizers

Note: For information on storing unused water chestnuts, see page 7.

Top to Bottom: Spicy Chicken Bundles, Spring Rolls

Marinated Vegetables

MARINATED VEGETABLES

⅓ cup peanut or vegetable oil
3 tablespoons rice vinegar
2 tablespoons soy sauce
1 clove garlic, minced
1 teaspoon minced fresh ginger
½ teaspoon sugar
2 cups broccoli florets
2 cups cauliflower florets
2 cups diagonally sliced carrots (½-inch pieces)
½ pound fresh mushrooms
1 large red bell pepper, cut into 1-inch pieces
  Lettuce leaves (optional)

1. Combine oil, vinegar, soy sauce, garlic, ginger and sugar in large bowl.

2. To blanch broccoli, cauliflower and carrots, cook 1 minute in salted boiling water to cover. Plunge into cold water, then drain immediately. Toss with oil mixture while still warm. Cool to room temperature.

3. Add mushrooms and red pepper to bowl; toss to coat. Cover and marinate in refrigerator at least 4 hours or up to 24 hours. Drain vegetables; reserve marinade. Arrange vegetables on lettuce-lined platter. Serve chilled or at room temperature with wooden toothpicks. If desired, serve reserved marinade in small cup for dipping. *Makes 12 to 16 appetizer servings*

HOT AND SOUR SOUP

1 package (1 ounce) dried black Chinese mushrooms*
4 ounces firm tofu, drained
4 cups chicken broth
3 tablespoons white vinegar
2 tablespoons soy sauce
½ to 1 teaspoon hot chili oil
¼ teaspoon ground white pepper
1 cup shredded cooked pork, chicken or turkey
½ cup drained canned bamboo shoots, cut into thin strips
3 tablespoons water
2 tablespoons cornstarch
1 egg white, slightly beaten
¼ cup thinly sliced green onions or chopped cilantro
1 teaspoon Oriental sesame oil

1. Place mushrooms in small bowl; cover with warm water. Soak 20 minutes to soften. Drain; squeeze out excess water. Discard stems; slice caps. Press tofu lightly between paper towels; cut into ½-inch squares or triangles.

2. Combine broth, vinegar, soy sauce, chili oil and pepper in medium saucepan. Bring to a boil over high heat. Reduce heat to medium. Simmer 2 minutes.

3. Stir in mushrooms, tofu, pork and bamboo shoots; heat through.

4. Blend water into cornstarch in cup until smooth. Stir into soup. Cook and stir 4 minutes or until soup boils and thickens.

5. Remove from heat. Stirring constantly in one direction, slowly pour egg white in a thin stream into soup. Stir in onions and sesame oil. Ladle into soup bowls.
Makes 4 to 6 appetizer servings (about 6 cups)

Note: For information on storing unused bamboo shoots and tofu, see pages 6 and 7.

*Or, substitute 2 cups sliced fresh mushrooms. Omit soaking mushrooms in step 1.

MEATS

SPICY BEEF WITH NOODLES

1 package (1 ounce) dried black Chinese
    mushrooms*
6 tablespoons peanut or vegetable oil,
    divided
2 teaspoons minced fresh ginger
2 large cloves garlic, minced
½ teaspoon crushed red pepper flakes
1 boneless beef top sirloin steak, cut
    1 inch thick (about 1 pound)
2 tablespoons soy sauce
2 tablespoons rice vinegar
1 teaspoon Oriental sesame oil
1 red bell pepper, cut into short, thin
    strips
5 ounces (1½-cups) fresh snow peas, cut
    lengthwise into thin strips
8 ounces vermicelli or thin spaghetti,
    broken in half *or* somen noodles,
    cooked and drained
    Coarsely chopped roasted cashews
    (optional)

1. Place mushrooms in small bowl; cover with warm water. Soak 30 minutes to soften. Drain; squeeze out excess water. Discard stems; slice caps.

2. Combine 2 tablespoons peanut oil, ginger, garlic and crushed red pepper in small bowl. Spread 2 teaspoons oil mixture evenly over both sides of steak. Marinate at room temperature 15 minutes or cover and refrigerate up to 24 hours. Stir soy sauce, vinegar, 3 tablespoons peanut oil and sesame oil into remaining oil mixture; set aside.

3. Heat large, deep nonstick skillet over medium to medium-high heat until hot. Add steak; cook 4 to 5 minutes per side.** Let stand on cutting board 10 minutes.

4. Heat remaining 1 tablespoon peanut oil in skillet over medium heat. Add mushrooms, red bell pepper and snow peas; stir-fry 3 to 4 minutes until vegetables are crisp-tender.

5. Toss hot cooked vermicelli with reserved oil mixture in large bowl. Cut steak across the grain into ⅛-inch slices; cut each slice into 1½-inch pieces. Add steak along with any accumulated juices to noodle mixture. Add vegetables; toss well. Serve warm, at room temperature or chilled. Just before serving, sprinkle with cashews. *Makes 4 to 6 servings*

*Or, substitute 4 ounces fresh shiitake mushrooms; discard stems and slice caps. Omit step 1.

**Cooking time is for medium-rare doneness. Adjust time for desired doneness.

Spicy Beef with Noodles

Barbecued Ribs

BARBECUED RIBS

3 to 4 pounds lean pork baby back ribs or spareribs
⅓ cup hoisin sauce
4 tablespoons soy sauce, divided
3 tablespoons dry sherry
3 cloves garlic, minced
2 tablespoons honey
1 tablespoon Oriental sesame oil

1. Place ribs in large plastic bag. Combine hoisin sauce, 3 tablespoons soy sauce, sherry and garlic in cup; pour over ribs. Close bag securely; turn to coat. Marinate in refrigerator at least 4 hours or up to 24 hours.

2. Preheat oven to 375°F. Drain ribs; reserve marinade. Place ribs on rack in shallow, foil-lined roasting pan. Cook 30 minutes. Turn; brush ribs with half of reserved marinade. Cook 15 minutes. Turn ribs over; brush with remaining marinade. Cook 15 minutes.

3. Combine remaining 1 tablespoon soy sauce, honey and sesame oil in small bowl; brush over ribs. Cook 5 to 10 minutes until ribs are browned and crisp.* Cut into serving-size pieces.

Makes 4 main-dish or 8 appetizer servings

*Ribs may be made ahead to this point; cover and refrigerate ribs up to 3 days. To reheat ribs, wrap in foil; cook in preheated 350°F oven 40 minutes or until heated through. Cut into serving-size pieces.

ROASTED PORK

3 tablespoons hoisin sauce
1 tablespoon soy sauce
1 tablespoon dry sherry
2 cloves garlic, minced
½ teaspoon crushed Szechuan peppercorns
    or crushed red pepper flakes
2 whole pork tenderloin roasts (about
    1¼ to 1½ pounds total weight)

1. Preheat oven to 350°F. Combine hoisin sauce, soy sauce, sherry, garlic and peppercorns in small bowl.

2. Brush one fourth of hoisin sauce mixture evenly over each roast. Place roasts on rack in shallow, foil-lined roasting pan. Cook roasts 15 minutes; turn and brush with remaining hoisin sauce mixture. Continue to cook until internal temperature reaches 155°F on meat thermometer inserted in thickest part of pork. (Timing will depend on thickness of pork; test at 30 minutes.)

3. Let pork stand, tented with foil, on cutting board 5 minutes. (Temperature of pork will rise to 160°F.) Slice diagonally and serve warm. Or, for use in other recipes, cut into portions and refrigerate up to 3 days or freeze up to 3 months.

Makes 4 to 6 servings

Variation: For *Chinese Barbecued Pork,* add 1 teaspoon red food coloring to hoisin sauce mixture. Prepare roasts as directed in recipe. Roasts may be grilled over medium coals until an internal temperature reaches 155°F on meat thermometer. (Turn pork after 8 minutes; check temperature at 16 minutes.)

SESAME–GARLIC FLANK STEAK

1 beef flank steak (about 1¼ pounds)
2 tablespoons soy sauce
2 tablespoons hoisin sauce
1 tablespoon Oriental sesame oil
2 cloves garlic, minced

1. Score steak lightly with a sharp knife in a diamond pattern on both sides; place in large plastic bag.

2. Combine remaining ingredients in small bowl; pour over steak. Close bag securely; turn to coat. Marinate in refrigerator at least 2 hours or up to 24 hours, turning once.

3. Drain steak; reserve marinade. Brush steak with some of the marinade. Grill or broil 5 to 6 inches from heat 5 minutes. Brush with marinade; turn steak over. Discard remaining marinade. Grill or broil 5 to 7 minutes until internal temperature reaches 135°F on meat thermometer inserted in thickest part of steak.* Carve steak across the grain into thin slices.   *Makes 4 servings*

*Broiling time is for medium-rare doneness. Adjust time for desired doneness.

CANTON PORK STEW

1½ pounds lean pork shoulder or pork loin
    roast, cut into 1-inch pieces
1 teaspoon ground ginger
¼ teaspoon ground cinnamon
¼ teaspoon ground red pepper
1 tablespoon peanut or vegetable oil
1 large onion, coarsely chopped
3 cloves garlic, minced
1 can (about 14 ounces) chicken broth
¼ cup dry sherry
1 package (about 10 ounces) frozen baby
    carrots, thawed
1 large green bell pepper, cut into 1-inch
    pieces
3 tablespoons soy sauce
1½ tablespoons cornstarch
    Cilantro for garnish

1. Sprinkle pork with ginger, cinnamon and ground red pepper; toss well. Heat large saucepan or Dutch oven over medium-high heat. Add oil; heat until hot.

2. Add pork to saucepan; brown on all sides. Add onion and garlic; cook 2 minutes, stirring frequently. Add broth and sherry. Bring to a boil over high heat. Reduce heat to medium-low. Cover and simmer 40 minutes.

3. Stir in carrots and green pepper; cover and simmer 10 minutes or until pork is fork tender. Blend soy sauce into cornstarch in cup until smooth. Stir into stew. Cook and stir 1 minute or until stew boils and thickens. Ladle into soup bowls. Garnish with cilantro. *Makes 6 servings*

BEEF WITH OYSTER SAUCE

1 tablespoon soy sauce
2 cloves garlic, minced
¼ to ½ teaspoon crushed red pepper
    flakes
1 boneless beef top sirloin or tenderloin
    steak, cut 1 inch thick (about
    1 pound)
½ cup chicken broth
¼ cup oyster sauce
1 tablespoon cornstarch
1 tablespoon peanut or vegetable oil
3 thin green onions, cut diagonally into
    1-inch pieces
1 teaspoon sesame seeds for garnish
    (optional)
    Hot cooked white rice (optional)

1. Combine soy sauce, garlic and crushed red pepper in medium bowl. Cut beef across the grain into ¼-inch slices; cut each slice into 2-inch pieces. Toss beef with soy sauce mixture. Marinate at room temperature 20 minutes or cover and refrigerate up to 8 hours.

2. Blend broth and oyster sauce into cornstarch in cup until smooth.

3. Heat wok or large skillet over medium-high heat. Add oil; heat until hot. Add half of beef mixture; stir-fry until beef is barely pink in center. Remove and reserve. Repeat with remaining beef mixture; remove and reserve.

4. Stir broth mixture and add to wok along with onions. Stir-fry 1 minute or until sauce boils and thickens.

5. Return beef along with any accumulated juices to wok; heat through. Garnish with sesame seeds. Serve with rice.
Makes 4 servings

Canton Pork Stew

Pepper Beef

PEPPER BEEF

1 tablespoon soy sauce
2 cloves garlic, minced
¼ teaspoon crushed red pepper flakes
1 boneless beef sirloin, tenderloin or rib
   eye steak, cut 1 inch thick (about
   1 pound)
2 tablespoons peanut or vegetable oil,
   divided
1 small red bell pepper, cut into thin
   strips
1 small yellow or green bell pepper, cut
   into thin strips
1 small onion, cut into thin strips
¼ cup stir-fry sauce
2 tablespoons rice wine or dry white wine
¼ cup coarsely chopped cilantro
   Hot cooked white rice or Chinese egg
   noodles (optional)

1. Combine soy sauce, garlic and crushed red pepper in medium bowl. Cut beef across the grain into ⅛-inch slices; cut each slice into 1½-inch pieces. Toss beef with soy sauce mixture.

2. Heat wok or large skillet over medium-high heat. Add 1 tablespoon oil; heat until hot. Add half of beef mixture; stir-fry until beef is barely pink in center. Remove and reserve. Repeat with remaining beef mixture; remove and reserve.

3. Heat remaining 1 tablespoon oil in wok; add bell peppers and onion. Reduce heat to medium. Stir-fry 6 to 7 minutes until vegetables are crisp-tender. Add stir-fry sauce and wine; stir-fry 2 minutes or until heated through.

4. Return beef along with any accumulated juices to wok; heat through. Sprinkle with cilantro. Serve over rice.

Makes 4 servings

LEMON–ORANGE GLAZED RIBS

2 whole slabs baby back pork ribs, cut
   into halves (about 3 pounds)
2 tablespoons soy sauce
2 tablespoons orange juice
2 tablespoons fresh lemon juice
2 cloves garlic, minced
¼ cup orange marmalade
1 tablespoon hoisin sauce

1. Place ribs in large plastic bag. Combine soy sauce, orange and lemon juices and garlic in small bowl; pour over ribs. Close bag securely; turn to coat. Marinate in refrigerator at least 4 hours or up to 24 hours, turning once.

2. Preheat oven to 350°F. Drain ribs; reserve marinade. Place ribs on rack in shallow, foil-lined roasting pan. Brush half of marinade evenly over ribs: bake 20 minutes. Turn ribs over; brush with remaining marinade. Bake 20 minutes.

3. Remove ribs from oven; pour off drippings. Combine marmalade and hoisin sauce in cup; brush half of mixture over ribs. Return to oven; bake 10 minutes or until glazed. Turn ribs over; brush with remaining marmalade mixture. Bake 10 minutes more or until ribs are browned and glazed. *Makes 4 servings*

HONEY–GLAZED PORK

1 large *or* 2 small pork tenderloins (about
    1¼ pounds total weight)
¼ cup soy sauce
2 cloves garlic, minced
3 tablespoons honey
2 tablespoons brown sugar
1 teaspoon minced fresh ginger
1 tablespoon toasted sesame seeds*

1. Place pork in large plastic bag. Combine soy sauce and garlic in small cup; pour over pork. Close bag securely; turn to coat. Marinate in refrigerator up to 2 hours.

2. Preheat oven to 400°F. Drain pork; reserve 1 tablespoon marinade. Combine honey, brown sugar, ginger and reserved marinade in small bowl.

3. Place pork in shallow, foil-lined roasting pan. Brush with half of honey mixture. Roast 10 minutes. Turn pork over; brush with remaining honey mixture and sprinkle with sesame seeds. Roast 10 minutes for small or 15 minutes for large tenderloin or until internal temperature reaches 155°F when tested with a meat thermometer inserted in thickest part of pork.

4. Let pork stand, tented with foil, on cutting board 5 minutes. (Temperature will rise to 160°F.) Pour pan juices into serving pitcher. Cut pork across the grain into ½-inch slices. Serve with pan juices. *Makes 4 servings*

*To toast sesame seeds, spread seeds in small skillet. Shake skillet over medium heat 2 minutes or until seeds begin to pop and turn golden.

MEAT PATTIES WITH CHINESE GRAVY

1 pound lean ground beef
¼ cup fresh bread crumbs
3 tablespoons minced onion
3 tablespoons chopped cilantro, divided
2 tablespoons oyster sauce
2 cloves garlic, minced
1 cup beef broth
1 tablespoon cornstarch
¼ teaspoon sugar
¼ teaspoon crushed red pepper flakes
    (optional)
    Hot cooked white rice (optional)

1. Combine ground beef, bread crumbs, onion, 2 tablespoons cilantro, oyster sauce and garlic in medium bowl. Mix lightly, but thoroughly. Shape to form 4 oval patties, ½ inch thick.

2. Heat large nonstick skillet over medium heat. Add patties; cook 7 minutes. Turn patties over; cook 6 to 7 minutes.*

3. Remove patties to warm serving platter. Spoon off fat from skillet, if necessary. Blend broth into cornstarch in small bowl until smooth. Pour into skillet along with sugar and crushed red pepper. Cook and stir 1 minute or until sauce boils and thickens; pour over patties. Sprinkle with remaining 1 tablespoon cilantro. Serve with rice. *Makes 4 servings*

*Cooking time is for medium doneness. Adjust time for desired doneness.

MONGOLIAN HOT POT

2 ounces bean threads
1 boneless beef sirloin or tenderloin steak,
    cut 1 inch thick (about ½ pound)
1 can (46 ounces) chicken broth
½ pound pork tenderloin, cut into ⅛-inch
    slices
½ pound medium raw shrimp, peeled,
    deveined
½ pound sea scallops, cut lengthwise into
    halves
½ pound small fresh mushrooms
    Dipping Sauce (recipe follows)
1 pound spinach leaves

1. Place bean threads in medium bowl; cover with warm water. Soak 15 minutes to soften; drain well. Cut bean threads into 1- to 2-inch lengths; set aside.

2. Cut beef across the grain into ⅛-inch slices; cut each slice into 1½-inch pieces.

3. Heat broth in electric skillet to a simmer (or, heat half of broth in fondue pot, keeping remaining broth hot for replacement).

4. Arrange beef, pork, shrimp, scallops and mushrooms on large platter.

5. Prepare Dipping Sauce.

6. To serve, select food from platter and cook it in simmering broth until desired doneness, using chop sticks or long-handled fork. Dip into dipping sauce before eating.

7. After all the food is cooked, stir spinach into broth and heat until wilted. (Cook spinach in two batches if using a fondue pot.) Place bean threads in individual soup bowls. Ladle broth mixture into bowls. Season with dipping sauce, if desired.

Makes 4 to 6 servings

DIPPING SAUCE

Combine ½ cup lite soy sauce, ¼ cup dry sherry and 1 tablespoon Oriental sesame oil in small bowl; divide into individual dipping bowls.

ORANGE BEEF

1 boneless beef sirloin or tenderloin steak,
    cut 1 inch thick (about 1 pound)
2 cloves garlic, minced
1 teaspoon grated *fresh* orange peel
2 tablespoons soy sauce
2 tablespoons orange juice
1 tablespoon dry sherry
1 tablespoon cornstarch
1 tablespoon peanut or vegetable oil
2 cups hot cooked white rice (optional)
    Orange slices for garnish

1. Cut beef across the grain into ⅛-inch slices; cut each slice into 2-inch pieces. Toss with garlic and orange peel in medium bowl.

2. Blend soy sauce, orange juice and sherry into cornstarch in cup until smooth.

3. Heat wok or large skillet over medium-high heat. Add oil; heat until hot. Add beef mixture; stir-fry 2 to 3 minutes or until beef is barely pink in center. Stir soy sauce mixture and add to wok. Stir-fry 30 seconds or until sauce boils and thickens. Serve over rice. Garnish with orange slices.

Makes 4 servings

GINGER BEEF

3 tablespoons soy sauce
2 cloves garlic, minced
1 tablespoon minced fresh ginger
¼ teaspoon crushed red pepper flakes
1 beef tenderloin or boneless beef sirloin
    steak, cut 1 inch thick (about
    1 pound)
¾ cup beef or chicken broth
3½ teaspoons cornstarch
2 tablespoons peanut or vegetable oil,
    divided
1 large yellow onion or sweet onion, cut
    into thin wedges
½ teaspoon sugar
    Hot cooked white rice (optional)
¼ cup coarsely chopped cilantro or sliced
    green onions for garnish

1. Combine soy sauce, garlic, ginger and crushed red pepper in medium bowl. Cut beef across the grain into ⅛-inch slices; cut each slice into 1½-inch pieces. Toss beef with soy sauce mixture. Marinate at room temperature 20 minutes or cover and refrigerate up to 4 hours.

2. Blend broth into cornstarch in cup until smooth.

3. Heat wok or large skillet over medium heat. Add 1 tablespoon oil; heat until hot. Add onion; stir-fry 5 minutes. Sprinkle sugar over onion; cook 5 minutes more or until onion is light golden brown, stirring occasionally. Remove and reserve.

4. Heat remaining 1 tablespoon oil in wok over medium-high heat until hot. Drain beef; reserve marinade. Add beef to wok; stir-fry until beef is barely pink in center. Return onion to wok. Stir broth mixture and add to wok along with reserved marinade. Stir-fry 1 minute or until sauce boils and thickens. Serve over rice. Garnish with cilantro. *Makes 4 servings*

SWEET AND SOUR PORK

1 tablespoon soy sauce
2 cloves garlic, minced
1 lean boneless pork loin or tenderloin
    roast* (about 1 pound)
1 can (8 ounces) pineapple chunks in
    juice, undrained
2 tablespoons peanut or vegetable oil,
    divided
2 medium carrots, diagonally cut into thin
    slices
1 large green bell pepper, cut into 1-inch
    pieces
⅓ cup stir-fry sauce
1 tablespoon white wine or white vinegar
    Hot cooked white rice (optional)

1. Combine soy sauce and garlic in medium bowl. Cut pork across the grain into 1-inch pieces; toss with soy sauce mixture.

2. Drain pineapple; reserve 2 tablespoons juice.

3. Heat wok or large skillet over medium-high heat. Add 1 tablespoon oil; heat until hot. Add pork mixture; stir-fry 4 to 5 minutes until pork is no longer pink. Remove and reserve.

4. Heat remaining 1 tablespoon oil in wok. Add carrots and green pepper; stir-fry 4 to 5 minutes until vegetables are crisp-tender. Add pineapple; heat through.

5. Add stir-fry sauce, reserved pineapple juice and vinegar; stir-fry 30 seconds or until sauce boils.

6. Return pork along with any accumulated juices to wok; heat through. Serve over rice. *Makes 4 servings*

*Or, substitute 1 pound boneless skinless chicken breasts or thighs.

Beef and Broccoli

BEEF AND BROCCOLI

1 boneless beef top sirloin or tenderloin
   steak, cut 1 inch thick (about
   1 pound)
2 teaspoons minced fresh ginger
2 cloves garlic, minced
1 tablespoon peanut or vegetable oil
3 cups broccoli florets
¼ cup water
⅓ cup stir-fry sauce
   Hot cooked white rice (optional)

1. Cut beef across the grain into ⅛-inch slices; cut each slice into 1½-inch pieces. Toss beef with ginger and garlic in medium bowl.

2. Heat wok or large skillet over medium-high heat. Add oil; heat until hot. Add beef mixture; stir-fry 3 to 4 minutes until beef is barely pink in center. Remove and reserve.

3. Add broccoli and water to wok; cover and steam 3 to 5 minutes until broccoli is crisp-tender.

4. Return beef along with any accumulated juices to wok. Add stir-fry sauce. Cook until heated through. Serve over rice.

Makes 4 servings

Pork with Three Onions

PORK WITH THREE ONIONS

⅓ cup teriyaki sauce
2 cloves garlic, minced
1 pound pork tenderloin
2 tablespoons peanut or vegetable oil,
    divided
1 small red onion, cut into thin wedges
1 small yellow onion, cut into thin wedges
1 teaspoon sugar
1 teaspoon cornstarch
2 green onions, cut into 1-inch pieces
    Fried bean threads* (optional)

1. Combine teriyaki sauce and garlic in shallow bowl. Cut pork across the grain into ¼-inch slices; cut each slice in half. Toss pork with teriyaki mixture. Marinate at room temperature 10 minutes.

2. Heat large skillet over medium-high heat. Add 1 tablespoon oil; heat until hot. Drain pork; reserve marinade. Stir-fry pork 3 minutes or until no longer pink. Remove and reserve.

3. Heat remaining 1 tablespoon oil in skillet; add red and yellow onions. Reduce heat to medium. Cook 4 to 5 minutes until softened, stirring occasionally. Sprinkle with sugar; cook 1 minute more.

4. Blend reserved marinade into cornstarch in cup until smooth. Stir into skillet. Stir-fry 1 minute or until sauce boils and thickens.

5. Return pork along with any accumulated juices to skillet; heat through. Stir in green onions. Serve over bean threads.

Makes 4 servings

*To fry bean threads, follow package directions.

FRAGRANT BEEF WITH GARLIC SAUCE

1 boneless beef top sirloin steak, cut
    1 inch thick (about 1¼ pounds)
⅓ cup teriyaki sauce
10 large cloves garlic, peeled
½ cup beef broth

1. Place beef in large plastic bag. Pour teriyaki sauce over beef. Close bag securely; turn to coat. Marinate in refrigerator at least 30 minutes or up to 4 hours.

2. Combine garlic and broth in small saucepan. Bring to a boil over high heat. Reduce heat to medium. Simmer, uncovered, 5 minutes. Cover and simmer 8 to 9 minutes until garlic is softened. Transfer to blender or food processor; process until smooth.

3. Meanwhile, drain beef; reserve marinade. Place beef on rack of broiler pan. Brush with half of reserved marinade. Broil 5 to 6 inches from heat 5 minutes. Turn beef over; brush with remaining marinade. Broil 5 minutes.*

4. Slice beef thinly; serve with garlic sauce.   *Makes 4 servings*

*Broiling time is for medium-rare doneness. Adjust time for desired doneness.

BEEF WITH LEEKS AND TOFU

8 ounces boneless beef sirloin, top loin or tenderloin steak, cut 1 inch thick

2 cloves garlic, minced

8 ounces firm tofu, drained

¾ cup chicken broth

¼ cup soy sauce

1 tablespoon dry sherry

1 tablespoon cornstarch

4 teaspoons peanut or vegetable oil, divided

1 large *or* 2 medium leeks, sliced (white and light green portion)

1 large red bell pepper, cut into short, thin strips

1 tablespoon Oriental sesame oil (optional)

Hot cooked spaghetti (optional)

1. Cut beef across the grain into ⅛-inch slices; cut each slice into 2-inch pieces. Toss beef with garlic in medium bowl. Press tofu lightly between paper towels; cut into ¾-inch triangles or squares.

2. Blend broth, soy sauce and sherry into cornstarch in small bowl until smooth.

3. Heat large, deep skillet over medium-high heat. Add 2 teaspoons peanut oil; heat until hot. Add beef mixture; stir-fry 2 to 2½ minutes until beef is barely pink in center. Remove and reserve.

4. Add remaining 2 teaspoons peanut oil to skillet. Add leek and red pepper; stir-fry 3 minutes or until red pepper is crisp-tender. Stir broth mixture and add to skillet along with tofu. Stir-fry 2 minutes or until sauce boils and thickens and tofu is hot, stirring frequently.

5. Return beef along with any accumulated juices to skillet; heat through. Stir in sesame oil. Serve over spaghetti.

Makes 4 servings

Note: For information on storing unused tofu, see page 7.

STIR–FRIED PORK AND VEGETABLES

1 pound lean boneless pork loin or tenderloin roast

2 cloves garlic, minced

2 teaspoons minced fresh ginger

2 tablespoons peanut or vegetable oil, divided

1 jar (7 ounces) baby corn cobs, drained and rinsed

6 ounces (2 cups) fresh snow peas *or* 1 package (6 ounces) frozen snow peas, thawed and cut into halves, if large

½ cup stir-fry sauce

Hot cooked white rice or Chinese egg noodles (optional)

1. Cut pork across the grain into ¼-inch slices; cut each slice into 1¼×¼-inch strips. Toss pork with garlic and ginger in small bowl.

2. Heat wok or large skillet over medium-high heat. Add 1 tablespoon oil; heat until hot. Add pork mixture; stir-fry 3 minutes or until pork is no longer pink. Remove and reserve.

3. Heat remaining 1 tablespoon oil in wok. Add corn cobs and snow peas; stir-fry 3 minutes for fresh or 2 minutes for frozen snow peas or until crisp-tender and corn cobs are hot. Add stir-fry sauce; stir-fry 30 seconds or until sauce boils.

4. Return pork along with any accumulated juices to wok; heat through. Serve over rice.

Makes 4 servings

POULTRY

GINGERED CHICKEN THIGHS

1 tablespoon peanut or vegetable oil
½ teaspoon hot chili oil
8 chicken thighs (1½ to 2 pounds)
2 cloves garlic, minced
¼ cup sweet and sour sauce
1 tablespoon soy sauce
2 teaspoons minced fresh ginger
　Cilantro and strips of orange peel for
　　garnish

1. Heat large nonstick skillet over medium-high heat. Add peanut oil and chili oil; heat until hot. Cook chicken, skin side down, 4 minutes or until golden brown.

2. Reduce heat to low; turn chicken skin side up. Cover and cook 15 to 18 minutes until juices run clear.

3. Spoon off fat. Increase heat to medium. Stir in garlic and cook 2 minutes. Combine sweet and sour sauce, soy sauce and ginger. Brush half of mixture over chicken; turn chicken over. Brush remaining mixture over chicken. Cook 5 minutes, turning once more, until sauce has thickened and chicken is browned. Transfer chicken to serving platter; pour sauce evenly over chicken. Garnish with cilantro and orange peel.　　*Makes 4 servings*

CRISPY ROASTED CHICKEN

1 roasting chicken or capon (about
　　6½ pounds)
1 tablespoon peanut or vegetable oil
2 cloves garlic, minced
1 tablespoon soy sauce

1. Preheat oven to 350°F. Rinse chicken; pat dry. Place on rack in shallow, foil-lined roasting pan.

2. Combine oil and garlic in small cup; brush evenly over chicken. Roast 15 to 20 minutes per pound or until internal temperature reaches 170°F on meat thermometer inserted in thickest part of thigh.

3. Increase oven temperature to 450°F. Remove drippings from pan; discard. Brush chicken evenly with soy sauce. Roast 5 to 10 minutes until skin is very crisp and deep golden brown. Let stand on cutting board 10 minutes. Cover and refrigerate leftovers up to 3 days or freeze up to 3 months.　　*Makes 8 to 10 servings*

Gingered Chicken Thighs

HONEY–LIME GLAZED CHICKEN

1 broiler-fryer chicken, quartered (about
 3½ pounds) *or* 3 pounds chicken
 parts
 ⅓ cup honey
 2 tablespoons fresh lime juice
1½ tablespoons soy sauce

1. Preheat oven to 375°F. Arrange chicken, skin side up, in single layer in shallow casserole dish or 11×7-inch baking dish.

2. Combine remaining ingredients in small bowl; mix well. Brush one third of honey mixture over chicken; bake 15 minutes.

3. Brush one third of honey mixture over chicken; bake 15 minutes. Brush remaining honey mixture over chicken; bake 10 to 15 minutes until juices run clear. Transfer chicken to serving platter. If desired, spoon fat from juices in baking dish; serve juices with chicken.   *Makes 4 servings*

Almond Chicken

ALMOND CHICKEN

⅓ cup blanched whole almonds
1 pound boneless skinless chicken breasts
   or thighs
2 cloves garlic, minced
1 teaspoon minced fresh ginger
¼ teaspoon crushed red pepper flakes
¾ cup chicken broth
¼ cup soy sauce
4 teaspoons cornstarch
4 large ribs bok choy (about ¾ pound)
2 tablespoons peanut or vegetable oil,
   divided
2 medium carrots, thinly sliced
   Chow mein noodles or hot cooked white
   rice

1. Preheat oven to 350°F. Spread almonds on baking sheet. Toast 6 to 7 minutes until golden brown, stirring once. Set aside.

2. Cut chicken into 1-inch pieces. Toss chicken with garlic, ginger and crushed red pepper in medium bowl. Marinate chicken at room temperature 15 minutes.

3. Blend broth and soy sauce into cornstarch in small bowl until smooth.

4. Cut woody stems from bok choy leaves; slice stems into ½-inch pieces. Cut tops of leaves crosswise into halves.

5. Heat wok or large skillet over medium-high heat. Add 1 tablespoon oil; heat until hot. Add chicken mixture; stir-fry 3 minutes or until chicken is no longer pink. Remove and reserve.

6. Heat remaining 1 tablespoon oil in wok; add bok choy stems and carrots. Stir-fry 5 minutes or until vegetables are crisp-tender. Stir broth mixture and add to wok along with bok choy leaves. Stir-fry 1 minute or until sauce boils and thickens.

7. Return chicken along with any accumulated juices to wok; heat through. Stir in almonds. Serve over chow mein noodles.

Makes 4 servings

KUNG PO CHICKEN

1 pound boneless skinless chicken breasts
   or thighs
2 cloves garlic, minced
1 teaspoon hot chili oil
¼ cup lite soy sauce
2 teaspoons cornstarch
1 tablespoon peanut or vegetable oil
⅓ cup roasted peanuts
2 green onions, cut into short, thin strips
   Lettuce leaves (optional)
   Plum sauce (optional)

1. Cut chicken into 1-inch pieces. Toss chicken with garlic and chili oil in medium bowl.

2. Blend soy sauce into cornstarch in cup until smooth.

3. Heat wok or large skillet over medium-high heat. Add peanut oil; heat until hot. Add chicken mixture; stir-fry 3 minutes or until chicken is no longer pink.

4. Stir soy sauce mixture and add to wok along with peanuts and onions. Stir-fry 1 minute or until sauce boils and thickens.

5. To serve, spread each lettuce leaf lightly with plum sauce. Add chicken mixture; roll up and serve immediately.

Makes 4 main-dish or 8 appetizer servings

ORANGE–GINGER BROILED CORNISH HENS

2 large Cornish hens, split (about
    1½ pounds each)
2 teaspoons peanut or vegetable oil,
    divided
¼ cup orange marmalade
1 tablespoon minced fresh ginger

1. Place hens, skin side up, on rack of foil-lined broiler pan. Brush with 1 teaspoon oil.

2. Broil 6 to 7 inches from heat 10 minutes. Turn hens skin side down; brush with remaining 1 teaspoon oil. Broil 10 minutes.

3. Combine marmalade and ginger in cup; brush half of mixture over hens. Broil 5 minutes.

4. Turn hens skin side up; brush with remaining marmalade mixture. Broil 5 minutes or until juices run clear and hens are browned and glazed. *Makes 4 servings*

CASHEW CHICKEN

1 pound boneless skinless chicken breasts
    or thighs
2 teaspoons minced fresh ginger
1 tablespoon peanut or vegetable oil
1 medium red bell pepper, cut into short,
    thin strips
⅓ cup teriyaki baste and glaze sauce
⅓ cup roasted or dry roasted cashews
    Hot cooked white rice (optional)
    Coarsely chopped cilantro (optional)

1. Cut chicken into ½-inch slices; cut each slice into 1½×½-inch strips. Toss chicken with ginger in small bowl.

2. Heat wok or large skillet over medium-high heat. Add oil; heat until hot. Add chicken mixture; stir-fry 2 minutes. Add red pepper; stir-fry 4 minutes or until chicken is no longer pink and red pepper is crisp-tender.

3. Add teriyaki sauce; stir-fry 1 minute or until sauce is hot. Stir in cashews. Serve over rice. Sprinkle with cilantro. *Makes 4 servings*

GARLICKY BAKED CHICKEN

1½ cups fresh bread crumbs
3 cloves garlic, minced
1 tablespoon peanut or vegetable oil
2 tablespoons soy sauce
1 tablespoon Chinese hot mustard
1 broiler-fryer chicken, cut up (about
    3½ pounds) *or* 3½ pounds chicken
    parts, skinned, if desired

1. Preheat oven to 350°F. Combine bread crumbs, garlic and oil in shallow dish.

2. Combine soy sauce and hot mustard in small bowl; brush evenly over chicken. Dip chicken in bread crumb mixture to coat lightly, but evenly. Place on foil-lined baking sheet.

3. Bake chicken 45 to 55 minutes until juices run clear. *Makes 4 to 6 servings*

Orange-Ginger Broiled Cornish Hens

Chicken Chow Mein

CHICKEN CHOW MEIN

1 pound boneless skinless chicken breasts
    or thighs
2 cloves garlic, minced
2 tablespoons peanut or vegetable oil,
    divided
¼ cup soy sauce
2 tablespoons dry sherry
6 ounces (2 cups) fresh snow peas *or*
    1 package (6 ounces) frozen snow
    peas, thawed, cut into halves
3 large green onions, cut diagonally into
    1-inch pieces
6 ounces uncooked Chinese egg noodles
    or vermicelli, cooked, drained and
    rinsed
1 tablespoon Oriental sesame oil

1. Cut chicken crosswise into ¼-inch slices; cut each slice into 1 × ¼-inch strips. Toss chicken with garlic in small bowl.

2. Heat wok or large skillet over medium-high heat. Add 1 tablespoon peanut oil; heat until hot. Add chicken mixture; stir-fry 3 minutes or until chicken is no longer pink. Transfer to bowl; toss with soy sauce and sherry.

3. Heat remaining 1 tablespoon peanut oil in wok. Add snow peas; stir-fry 2 minutes for fresh or 1 minute for frozen snow peas. Add onions; stir-fry 30 seconds. Add chicken mixture; stir-fry 1 minute.

4. Add noodles to wok; stir-fry 2 minutes or until heated through. Stir in sesame oil; serve immediately. *Makes 4 servings*

MOO GOO GAI PAN

1 package (1 ounce) dried black Chinese
    mushrooms
¼ cup lite soy sauce
2 tablespoons rice vinegar
3 cloves garlic, minced
1 pound boneless skinless chicken breasts
½ cup chicken broth
1 tablespoon cornstarch
2 tablespoons peanut or vegetable oil,
    divided
1 jar (7 ounces) straw mushrooms,
    drained
3 green onions, cut into 1-inch pieces
    Hot cooked white rice or Chinese egg
    noodles (optional)

1. Place dried mushrooms in small bowl; cover with warm water. Soak 30 minutes to soften. Drain; squeeze out excess water. Discard stems; slice caps.

2. Combine soy sauce, vinegar and garlic in medium bowl. Cut chicken crosswise into ½-inch strips. Toss chicken with soy sauce mixture. Marinate at room temperature 20 minutes.

3. Blend broth into cornstarch in cup until smooth.

4. Heat wok or large skillet over medium-high heat. Add 1 tablespoon oil; heat until hot. Drain chicken; reserve marinade. Add chicken to wok; stir-fry chicken 3 minutes or until no longer pink. Remove and reserve.

5. Heat remaining 1 tablespoon oil in wok; add dried and straw mushrooms and onions. Stir-fry 1 minute.

6. Stir broth mixture and add to wok along with reserved marinade. Stir-fry 1 minute or until sauce boils and thickens.

7. Return chicken along with any accumulated juices to wok; heat through. Serve over rice. *Makes 4 servings*

SZECHUAN CHICKEN SALAD WITH PEANUT DRESSING

1 pound boneless skinless chicken breast
  halves
1 can (about 14 ounces) chicken broth
1 tablespoon creamy peanut butter
1 tablespoon peanut or vegetable oil
1 tablespoon soy sauce
1 tablespoon rice vinegar
1 teaspoon Oriental sesame oil
¼ teaspoon ground red pepper
  Shredded lettuce
  Chopped cilantro or green onions
    (optional)

1. Place chicken in single layer in large skillet. Pour broth over chicken. Bring to a boil over high heat. Reduce heat to medium-low. Cover and simmer 10 to 12 minutes until chicken is no longer pink in center.

2. Meanwhile, mix peanut butter and peanut oil in small bowl until smooth. Stir in soy sauce, vinegar, sesame oil and ground red pepper.

3. Drain chicken; reserve broth. Stir 2 tablespoons of the reserved broth* into peanut butter mixture.

4. To serve salad warm, cut chicken crosswise into ½-inch slices and place on lettuce-lined plates. Spoon peanut dressing over chicken. Sprinkle with cilantro.

5. To serve salad at room temperature, cool chicken and shred or coarsely chop. Toss chicken with peanut dressing; cover and refrigerate. Just before serving, bring chicken mixture to room temperature (about 1 hour). Arrange chicken on lettuce-lined plates. Sprinkle with cilantro. *Makes 4 servings*

*Strain remaining broth; cover and refrigerate or freeze for use in other recipes.

HOISIN-ROASTED CHICKEN WITH VEGETABLES

1 broiler-fryer chicken, cut up (about
  3 pounds)
3 tablespoons hoisin sauce
1 tablespoon dry sherry
1 tablespoon Oriental sesame oil
6 ounces medium or large fresh
  mushrooms
2 small red or yellow onions, cut into thin
  wedges
1 package (9 or 10 ounces) frozen baby
  carrots, thawed

1. Preheat oven to 375°F. Place chicken, skin side up, in shallow, lightly oiled, foil-lined roasting pan.

2. Combine hoisin sauce, sherry and sesame oil in small bowl. Brush half of mixture evenly over chicken; bake 20 minutes.

3. Scatter mushrooms, onions and carrots around chicken. Brush remaining hoisin sauce mixture over chicken and vegetables; bake 20 minutes or until juices from chicken run clear.

Makes 4 to 6 servings

PINEAPPLE–HOISIN HENS

2 cloves garlic
1 can (8 ounces) crushed pineapple in juice, undrained
2 tablespoons rice vinegar
2 tablespoons soy sauce
2 tablespoons hoisin sauce
2 teaspoons minced fresh ginger
1 teaspoon Chinese five-spice powder
2 large Cornish hens (about 1½ pounds each), split in half

1. Mince garlic in blender or food processor. Add pineapple with juice; process until fairly smooth. Add remaining ingredients except hens; process 5 seconds.

2. Place hens in large plastic bag; pour pineapple mixture over hens. Close bag securely; turn to coat. Marinate in refrigerator at least 2 hours or up to 24 hours, turning bag once.

3. Preheat oven to 375°F. Drain hens; reserve marinade. Place hens, skin side up, on rack in shallow, foil-lined roasting pan. Roast 35 minutes.

4. Brush hens lightly with some of the reserved marinade; discard remaining marinade. Roast 10 minutes or until hens are browned and juices run clear. *Makes 4 servings*

ORIENTAL CHICKEN KABOBS

1 pound boneless skinless chicken breasts
2 small zucchini or yellow squash, cut into 1-inch slices
8 large fresh mushrooms
1 large red, yellow or green bell pepper, cut into 1-inch pieces
¼ cup soy sauce
2 tablespoons dry sherry
2 teaspoons Oriental sesame oil
2 cloves garlic, minced
2 large green onions, cut into 1-inch pieces

1. Cut chicken into 1½-inch pieces; place in large plastic bag. Add zucchini, mushrooms and red pepper to bag. Combine soy sauce, sherry, sesame oil and garlic in cup; pour over chicken and vegetables. Close bag securely; turn to coat. Marinate in refrigerator at least 30 minutes or up to 4 hours.

2. Drain chicken and vegetables; reserve marinade. Alternately thread chicken and vegetables with onions onto metal skewers.

3. Place kabobs on rack of broiler pan. Brush with half of reserved marinade. Broil 5 to 6 inches from heat 5 minutes. Turn kabobs over; brush with remaining marinade. Discard any remaining marinade. Broil 5 minutes or until chicken is no longer pink. *Makes 4 servings*

CHINESE CHICKEN SALAD

3 tablespoons peanut or vegetable oil
3 tablespoons rice vinegar
2 tablespoons soy sauce
1 tablespoon honey
1 teaspoon minced fresh ginger
1 teaspoon Oriental sesame oil
1 clove garlic, minced
¼ teaspoon crushed red pepper flakes
    (optional)
4 cups chopped cooked chicken or turkey
4 cups packed shredded napa cabbage or
    romaine lettuce
1 cup shredded carrots
½ cup thinly sliced green onions
1 can (5 ounces) chow mein noodles
    (optional)
¼ cup chopped cashews or peanuts
    (optional)
    Carrot curls and green onions for
    garnish

1. For dressing, combine peanut oil, vinegar, soy sauce, honey, ginger, sesame oil, garlic and crushed red pepper in small jar with tight-fitting lid; shake well.

2. Place chicken in large bowl. Pour dressing over chicken; toss to coat.*

3. Add cabbage, shredded carrots and sliced onions to bowl; toss well to coat. Serve over chow mein noodles. Sprinkle cashews over salad. Garnish with carrot curls and onions.
Makes 4 to 6 servings (about 8 cups salad)

*Salad may be made ahead to this point; cover and refrigerate chicken mixture until ready to serve.

CHICKEN CHOP SUEY

1 package (1 ounce) dried black Chinese
    mushrooms
3 tablespoons soy sauce
1 tablespoon cornstarch
1 pound boneless skinless chicken breasts
    or thighs
2 cloves garlic, minced
1 tablespoon peanut or vegetable oil
½ cup thinly sliced celery
½ cup sliced water chestnuts
½ cup bamboo shoots
1 cup chicken broth
    Hot cooked white rice or chow mein
    noodles
    Thinly sliced green onions (optional)

1. Place mushrooms in small bowl; cover with warm water. Soak 20 minutes to soften. Drain; squeeze out excess water. Discard stems; quarter caps.

2. Blend soy sauce into cornstarch in cup until smooth.

3. Cut chicken into 1-inch pieces; toss with garlic in small bowl. Heat wok or large skillet over medium-high heat. Add oil; heat until hot. Add chicken mixture and celery; stir-fry 2 minutes. Add water chestnuts and bamboo shoots; stir-fry 1 minute. Add broth and mushrooms; cook 3 minutes or until chicken is no longer pink in center, stirring frequently.

4. Stir soy sauce mixture and add to wok. Cook and stir 1 to 2 minutes until sauce boils and thickens. Serve over rice. Garnish with onions.
Makes 4 servings

Chinese Chicken Salad

Shanghai Chicken with Asparagus and Ham

SHANGHAI CHICKEN WITH ASPARAGUS AND HAM

2 cups diagonally cut 1-inch asparagus
    pieces*
1 pound boneless skinless chicken breasts
    or thighs
1 tablespoon peanut or vegetable oil
1 medium onion, coarsely chopped
2 cloves garlic, minced
¼ cup stir-fry sauce
½ cup diced deli ham
    Hot cooked Chinese egg noodles or
    white rice (optional)

1. To blanch asparagus pieces, cook 3 minutes in boiling water to cover. Plunge asparagus into cold water. Drain well.

2. Cut chicken crosswise into 1-inch pieces.

3. Heat wok or large skillet over medium-high heat. Add oil; heat until hot.

4. Add onion and garlic; stir-fry 2 minutes. Add chicken; stir-fry 2 minutes. Add asparagus; stir-fry 2 minutes or until chicken is no longer pink.

5. Add stir-fry sauce; mix well. Add ham; stir-fry until heated through. Serve over noodles. *Makes 4 servings*

*Or, substitute thawed frozen asparagus. Omit step 1.

CHINESE CURRIED CHICKEN

1 pound boneless skinless chicken breasts
    or thighs
1 tablespoon all-purpose flour
1 tablespoon curry powder
¼ teaspoon salt
¼ teaspoon ground red pepper
2 tablespoons peanut or vegetable oil,
    divided
1 large onion, chopped
2 cloves garlic, minced
1 can (14 ounces) coconut milk
3 tablespoons soy sauce
6 ounces (2 cups) fresh snow peas *or*
    1 package (6 ounces) frozen snow
    peas, thawed
    Hot cooked white rice or Chinese egg
    noodles
¼ cup chopped cilantro or thinly sliced
    green onions
2 tablespoons chopped peanuts or
    cashews

1. Cut chicken into 1-inch pieces. Combine flour, curry powder, salt and ground red pepper in medium plastic bag. Add chicken; shake to coat.

2. Heat large skillet over medium-high heat. Add 1 tablespoon oil; heat until hot. Add onion and garlic; cook 3 minutes, stirring occasionally.

3. Push onion mixture to edges of skillet. Add remaining 1 tablespoon oil and chicken mixture; stir-fry 2 to 3 minutes until chicken is no longer pink. Add coconut milk and soy sauce; reduce heat to medium-low. Simmer, uncovered, 10 minutes.

4. Stir in snow peas; cook 4 minutes for fresh or 2 minutes for frozen snow peas or until crisp-tender and sauce is slightly thickened. Serve over rice. Sprinkle with cilantro and peanuts.
Makes 4 servings

CHINESE CHICKEN STEW

1 package (1 ounce) dried black Chinese
    mushrooms
1 pound boneless skinless chicken thighs
1 teaspoon Chinese five-spice powder
¼ to ½ teaspoon crushed red pepper
    flakes
1 tablespoon peanut or vegetable oil
1 large onion, coarsely chopped
2 cloves garlic, minced
1 can (about 14 ounces) chicken broth,
    divided
1 tablespoon cornstarch
1 large red bell pepper, cut into ¾-inch
    pieces
1 tablespoon soy sauce
2 large green onions, cut into ½-inch
    pieces
1 tablespoon Oriental sesame oil
3 cups hot cooked white rice (optional)
¼ cup coarsely chopped cilantro (optional)

1. Place mushrooms in small bowl; cover with warm water. Soak 20 minutes to soften. Drain; squeeze out excess water. Discard stems; slice caps.

2. Cut chicken into 1-inch pieces. Toss chicken with five-spice powder in small bowl. Season to taste with crushed red pepper.

3. Heat wok or large skillet over medium-high heat. Add peanut oil; heat until hot. Add chicken mixture, chopped onion and garlic; stir-fry 2 minutes or until chicken is no longer pink.

4. Blend ¼ cup broth into cornstarch in cup until smooth.

5. Add remaining broth to wok. Stir red bell pepper, mushrooms and soy sauce into stew. Reduce heat to medium. Cover and simmer 10 minutes.

6. Stir cornstarch mixture and add to wok. Cook and stir 2 minutes or until sauce boils and thickens. Stir in green onions and sesame oil. Ladle into soup bowls; scoop ½ cup rice into each bowl. Sprinkle with cilantro.

Makes 6 servings (about 5 cups)

SESAME CHICKEN

1 pound boneless skinless chicken breasts
    or thighs
⅓ cup teriyaki sauce
2 teaspoons cornstarch
1 tablespoon peanut or vegetable oil
2 cloves garlic, minced
2 large green onions, cut into ½-inch
    slices
1 tablespoon toasted sesame seeds*
1 teaspoon Oriental sesame oil

1. Cut chicken into 1-inch pieces; toss chicken with teriyaki sauce in small bowl. Marinate at room temperature 15 minutes or cover and refrigerate up to 2 hours.

2. Drain chicken; reserve marinade. Blend reserved marinade into cornstarch in cup until smooth.

3. Heat wok or large skillet over medium-high heat. Add peanut oil; heat until hot. Add chicken and garlic; stir-fry 3 minutes or until chicken is no longer pink. Stir marinade mixture and add to wok along with onions and sesame seeds. Stir-fry 30 seconds or until sauce boils and thickens. Stir in sesame oil.

Makes 4 servings

*To toast sesame seeds, spread seeds in small skillet. Shake skillet over medium heat 2 minutes or until seeds begin to pop and turn golden.

Chinese Chicken Stew

CILANTRO–STUFFED CHICKEN BREASTS

2 cloves garlic
1 cup packed cilantro leaves
1 tablespoon *plus* 2 teaspoons soy sauce,
    divided
1 tablespoon peanut or vegetable oil
4 chicken breast halves (about
    1¼ pounds)
1 tablespoon Oriental sesame oil

1. Preheat oven to 350°F. Mince garlic in blender or food processor. Add cilantro; process until cilantro is minced. Add 2 teaspoons soy sauce and peanut oil; process until paste forms.

2. With rubber spatula or fingers, distribute about 1 tablespoon cilantro mixture evenly under skin of each chicken breast half, taking care not to puncture skin.

3. Place chicken on rack in shallow, foil-lined baking pan. Combine remaining 1 tablespoon soy sauce and sesame oil. Brush half of mixture evenly over chicken. Bake 25 minutes; brush remaining soy sauce mixture evenly over chicken. Bake 10 minutes or until juices run clear. *Makes 4 servings*

SEAFOOD

GRILLED CHINESE SALMON

3 tablespoons soy sauce
2 tablespoons dry sherry
2 cloves garlic, minced
1 pound salmon steaks or fillets
2 tablespoons finely chopped fresh
    cilantro

1. Combine soy sauce, sherry and garlic in shallow dish. Add salmon; turn to coat. Cover and refrigerate at least 30 minutes or up to 2 hours.

2. Drain salmon; reserve marinade. Arrange steaks (arrange fillets skin side down) on oiled rack of broiler pan or oiled grid over hot coals. Broil or grill 5 to 6 inches from heat 10 minutes. Baste with reserved marinade after 5 minutes of broiling; discard any remaining marinade. Sprinkle with cilantro.   *Makes 4 servings*

STIR–FRIED CRAB

8 ounces firm tofu, drained
1 tablespoon soy sauce
¼ cup chicken broth
3 tablespoons oyster sauce
2 teaspoons cornstarch
1 tablespoon peanut or vegetable oil
6 ounces (2 cups) fresh snow peas, cut
    into halves *or* 1 package (6 ounces)
    frozen snow peas, separated, but not
    thawed
8 ounces thawed frozen cooked crabmeat
    or imitation crabmeat, broken into
    ½-inch pieces (about 2 cups)
  Sesame Noodle Cake (page 224)
    (optional)
2 tablespoons chopped cilantro or thinly
    sliced green onions

1. Press tofu lightly between paper towels; cut into ½-inch squares or triangles. Place in shallow dish. Drizzle soy sauce over tofu.

2. Blend broth and oyster sauce into cornstarch in cup until smooth.

3. Heat wok or large skillet over medium-high heat. Add oil; heat until hot. Add snow peas; stir-fry 3 minutes for fresh or 2 minutes for frozen snow peas. Add crabmeat; stir-fry 1 minute. Stir broth mixture and add to wok. Stir-fry 30 seconds or until sauce boils and thickens.

4. Stir in tofu mixture; heat through. Serve over Sesame Noodle Cake. Sprinkle with cilantro.   *Makes 4 servings*

Note: For information on storing unused tofu, see page 7.

Grilled Chinese Salmon

Garlic Skewered Shrimp

GARLIC SKEWERED SHRIMP

1 pound large raw shrimp, peeled, deveined
2 tablespoons soy sauce
1 tablespoon peanut or vegetable oil
3 cloves garlic, minced
¼ teaspoon crushed red pepper flakes (optional)
3 green onions, cut into 1-inch pieces

1. Soak 4 (12-inch) bamboo skewers in water to cover 20 minutes.

2. Place shrimp in large plastic bag. Combine soy sauce, oil, garlic and crushed red pepper in cup; mix well. Pour over shrimp. Close bag securely; turn to coat. Marinate at room temperature 10 to 15 minutes.

3. Drain shrimp; reserve marinade. Alternately thread shrimp and onions onto skewers. Place on rack of broiler pan. Brush with reserved marinade; discard remaining marinade.

4. Broil shrimp 5 to 6 inches from heat 5 minutes. Turn shrimp over; broil 5 minutes or until shrimp are opaque.

Makes 4 servings

ORANGE–ALMOND SCALLOPS

3 tablespoons orange juice
3 tablespoons soy sauce
1 clove garlic, minced
1 pound bay scallops or halved sea scallops
1 tablespoon cornstarch
2 tablespoons peanut or vegetable oil, divided
1 green bell pepper, cut into short, thin strips
1 can (8 ounces) sliced water chestnuts, drained and rinsed
⅓ cup toasted blanched almonds
Hot cooked white rice (optional)
½ teaspoon finely grated orange peel

1. Combine orange juice, soy sauce and garlic in medium bowl. Add scallops; toss to coat. Marinate at room temperature 15 minutes or cover and refrigerate up to 1 hour.

2. Drain scallops; reserve marinade. Blend marinade into cornstarch in cup until smooth.

3. Heat wok or large skillet over medium-high heat. Add 1 tablespoon oil; heat until hot. Add scallops; stir-fry 2 minutes or until scallops are opaque. Remove and reserve.

4. Add remaining 1 tablespoon oil to wok. Add green pepper and water chestnuts. Stir-fry 3 minutes.

5. Return scallops along with any accumulated juices to wok. Stir marinade mixture and add to wok. Stir-fry 1 minute or until sauce boils and thickens. Stir in almonds. Serve over rice. Sprinkle with orange peel.

Makes 4 servings

BEIJING FILLET OF SOLE

2 tablespoons soy sauce
1 tablespoon Oriental sesame oil
4 sole fillets (6 ounces each)
1¼ cups preshredded coleslaw mix or
    cabbage
½ cup crushed chow mein noodles
1 egg white, slightly beaten
2 teaspoons toasted sesame seeds*

1. Preheat oven to 350°F. Combine soy sauce and sesame oil in small bowl. Place sole in shallow dish. Lightly brush both sides of sole with soy sauce mixture.

2. Combine coleslaw mix, noodles, egg white and remaining soy sauce mixture in small bowl. Spoon evenly over sole. Roll up each fillet and place, seam side down, in shallow, foil-lined roasting pan. Sprinkle rolls with sesame seeds. Bake 25 to 30 minutes until fish flakes easily when tested with fork.

Makes 4 servings

*To toast sesame seeds, spread seeds in small skillet. Shake skillet over medium heat 2 minutes or until seeds begin to pop and turn golden.

HOT AND SOUR SHRIMP

½ package (½ ounce) dried black Chinese
    mushrooms
½ small unpeeled cucumber
1 tablespoon brown sugar
2 teaspoons cornstarch
3 tablespoons rice vinegar
2 tablespoons soy sauce
1 tablespoon peanut or vegetable oil
1 pound medium raw shrimp, peeled,
    deveined
2 cloves garlic, minced
¼ teaspoon crushed red pepper flakes
1 large red bell pepper, cut into short,
    thin strips
    Hot cooked white rice or Chinese egg
    noodles (optional)

1. Place mushrooms in small bowl; cover with warm water. Soak 20 minutes to soften. Drain; squeeze out excess water. Discard stems; slice caps.

2. Cut cucumber in half lengthwise; scrape out seeds. Slice crosswise.

3. Combine brown sugar and cornstarch in small bowl. Blend in vinegar and soy sauce until smooth.

4. Heat wok or large skillet over medium-high heat. Add oil; heat until hot. Add shrimp, garlic and crushed red pepper; stir-fry 1 minute. Add mushrooms and red pepper strips; stir-fry 2 minutes or until shrimp are opaque.

5. Stir vinegar mixture and add to wok. Stir-fry 30 seconds or until sauce boils and thickens. Add cucumber; stir-fry until heated through. Serve over rice.

Makes 4 servings

Beijing Fillet of Sole

Easy Seafood Stir-Fry

EASY SEAFOOD STIR-FRY

1 package (1 ounce) dried black Chinese
    mushrooms*
1 cup chicken broth
3 tablespoons soy sauce
2 tablespoons dry sherry
4½ teaspoons cornstarch
2 tablespoons peanut or vegetable oil,
    divided
½ pound medium raw shrimp, peeled,
    deveined
½ pound bay scallops or halved sea
    scallops
2 cloves garlic, minced
6 ounces (2 cups) fresh snow peas, cut
    diagonally into halves
    Sesame Noodle Cake (page 224) *or* hot
    cooked white rice (optional)
¼ cup thinly sliced green onions (optional)

1. Place mushrooms in small bowl; cover with warm water. Soak 30 minutes to soften. Drain; squeeze out excess water. Discard stems; slice caps.

2. Blend broth, soy sauce and sherry into cornstarch in another small bowl until smooth.

3. Heat wok or large skillet over medium-high heat. Add 1 tablespoon oil; heat until hot. Add shrimp, scallops and garlic; stir-fry 3 minutes or until seafood is opaque. Remove and reserve.

4. Add remaining 1 tablespoon oil to wok. Add mushrooms and snow peas; stir-fry 3 minutes or until snow peas are crisp-tender.

5. Stir broth mixture and add to wok. Stir-fry 2 minutes or until sauce boils and thickens.

6. Return seafood along with any accumulated juices to wok; heat through. Serve over Sesame Noodle Cake. Garnish with onions. *Makes 4 servings*

*Or, substitute 1½ cups sliced fresh mushrooms. Omit step 1.

SHANGHAI STEAMED FISH

1 cleaned whole sea bass, red snapper,
    carp or grouper (about 1½ pounds)
¼ cup teriyaki sauce
2 teaspoons shredded fresh ginger
2 green onions, cut into 4-inch pieces
1 teaspoon Oriental sesame oil (optional)

1. Sprinkle inside cavity of fish with teriyaki sauce and ginger. Place onions in cavity in single layer.

2. Pour enough water into wok so that water is just below steaming rack. Bring water to a boil over high heat. Reduce heat to medium-low to maintain a simmer. Place fish on steaming rack in steamer. Cover and steam fish over simmering water about 10 minutes per inch of thickness measured at thickest part of fish. Fish is done when it flakes easily when tested with fork.

3. Carefully remove fish; discard onions. Cut fish into four serving-size portions. Sprinkle with sesame oil.
Makes 4 servings

BROILED HUNAN FISH FILLETS

3 tablespoons soy sauce
1 tablespoon finely chopped green onion
2 teaspoons Oriental sesame oil
1 teaspoon minced fresh ginger
1 clove garlic, minced
¼ teaspoon crushed red pepper flakes
1 pound red snapper, scrod or cod fillets

1. Combine soy sauce, onion, sesame oil, ginger, garlic and crushed pepper in cup.

2. Spray rack of broiler pan with nonstick cooking spray. Place fish on rack; brush with soy sauce mixture.

3. Broil 4 to 5 inches from heat 10 minutes or until fish flakes easily when tested with fork. *Makes 4 servings*

FIVE-SPICE SHRIMP WITH WALNUTS

1 pound medium or large raw shrimp,
    peeled, deveined
½ teaspoon Chinese five-spice powder
2 cloves garlic, minced
½ cup chicken broth
2 tablespoons soy sauce
2 tablespoons dry sherry
1 tablespoon cornstarch
1 tablespoon peanut or vegetable oil
1 large red bell pepper, cut into short,
    thin strips
⅓ cup walnut halves or quarters
    Hot cooked white rice (optional)
¼ cup thinly sliced green onions (optional)

1. Toss shrimp with five-spice powder and garlic in small bowl.

2. Blend broth, soy sauce and sherry into cornstarch in cup until smooth.

3. Heat wok or large skillet over medium-high heat. Add oil; heat until hot. Add shrimp mixture, red pepper and walnuts; stir-fry 3 to 5 minutes until shrimp are opaque and red pepper is crisp-tender.

4. Stir broth mixture and add to wok. Stir-fry 1 minute or until sauce boils and thickens. Serve over rice. Garnish with onions. *Makes 4 servings*

HALIBUT WITH CILANTRO AND LIME

1 pound halibut, tuna or swordfish steaks
2 tablespoons fresh lime juice
¼ cup regular or lite teriyaki sauce
1 teaspoon cornstarch
½ teaspoon minced fresh ginger
1 tablespoon peanut or vegetable oil
½ cup slivered red or yellow onion
2 cloves garlic, minced
¼ cup coarsely chopped cilantro

1. Cut halibut into 1-inch pieces; sprinkle with lime juice.

2. Blend teriyaki sauce into cornstarch in cup until smooth. Stir in ginger.

3. Heat wok or large skillet over medium-high heat. Add oil; heat until hot. Add onion and garlic; stir-fry 2 minutes. Add halibut; stir-fry 2 minutes or until halibut is opaque.

4. Stir teriyaki sauce mixture and add to wok. Stir-fry 30 seconds or until sauce boils and thickens. Sprinkle with cilantro. *Makes 4 servings*

Broiled Hunan Fish Fillets

VEGETABLES

DRAGON TOFU

¼ cup soy sauce
1 tablespoon creamy peanut butter
1 package (about 12 ounces) firm tofu, drained
1 medium zucchini squash
1 medium yellow squash
2 teaspoons peanut or vegetable oil
½ teaspoon hot chili oil
2 cloves garlic, minced
2 cups packed fresh torn spinach leaves
¼ cup coarsely chopped cashews or peanuts (optional)

1. Whisk soy sauce into peanut butter in small bowl. Press tofu lightly between paper towels; cut into ¾-inch squares or triangles. Place in single layer in shallow dish. Pour soy sauce mixture over tofu; stir gently to coat all surfaces. Let stand at room temperature 20 minutes.

2. Cut zucchini and yellow squash into ¼-inch slices; cut each slice into 2×¼-inch strips.

3. Heat nonstick skillet over medium-high heat. Add peanut oil and chili oil; heat until hot. Add garlic and squash; stir-fry 3 minutes. Add tofu mixture; cook 2 minutes or until tofu is heated through and sauce is slightly thickened, stirring occasionally.

4. Stir in spinach; remove from heat. Sprinkle with cashews.

Makes 2 main-dish or 4 side-dish servings

HOT AND SOUR ZUCCHINI

2 teaspoons minced fresh ginger
1 clove garlic, minced
¼ teaspoon crushed red pepper flakes or crushed Szechuan peppercorns
1 pound zucchini
2 teaspoons sugar
1 teaspoon cornstarch
2 tablespoons red wine vinegar
2 tablespoons soy sauce
1 tablespoon peanut or vegetable oil
1 teaspoon Oriental sesame oil

1. Combine ginger, garlic and crushed red pepper in small bowl. Cut zucchini into ¼-inch slices. If zucchini is large, cut each slice in half. Toss zucchini with ginger mixture.

2. Combine sugar and cornstarch in small bowl. Blend in vinegar and soy sauce until smooth.

3. Heat large nonstick skillet over medium-high heat. Add peanut oil; heat until hot. Add zucchini mixture; stir-fry 4 to 5 minutes until zucchini is crisp-tender.

4. Stir vinegar mixture and add to skillet. Stir-fry 15 seconds or until sauce boils and thickens. Stir in sesame oil.

Makes 4 servings

Dragon Tofu

Top to Bottom: Orange-Onion Salad, Roasted Shanghai Pepper Salad

ORANGE–ONION SALAD

1 tablespoon soy sauce
1 tablespoon rice vinegar
2 teaspoons Oriental sesame oil
1 large navel orange, peeled and sliced
1 small red onion, thinly sliced
   Romaine lettuce or spinach leaves
   Carrot curls for garnish

1. Combine soy sauce, vinegar and sesame oil in small bowl.

2. Place orange and onion slices in single layer in shallow baking dish; drizzle with soy sauce mixture. Cover and refrigerate at least 30 minutes or up to 8 hours.

3. Transfer orange and onion slices to lettuce-lined serving platter or individual lettuce-lined dishes; drizzle with juices from dish. Garnish with carrot curls.

Makes 4 servings

SZECHUAN–GRILLED MUSHROOMS

1 pound large fresh mushrooms
2 tablespoons soy sauce
2 teaspoons peanut or vegetable oil
1 teaspoon Oriental sesame oil
1 clove garlic, minced
½ teaspoon crushed Szechuan peppercorns
   or crushed red pepper flakes

1. Place mushrooms in large plastic bag. Add remaining ingredients to bag. Close bag securely; shake to coat mushrooms with marinade. Marinate at room temperature 15 minutes or cover and refrigerate up to 8 hours. (Mushrooms will absorb marinade.)

2. Thread mushrooms onto skewers. Grill or broil mushrooms 5 inches from heat 10 minutes or until lightly browned, turning once. Serve immediately.

Makes 4 servings

Variation: For *Szechuan-Grilled Mushrooms and Onions,* add 4 green onions, cut into 1½-inch pieces, to marinade. Alternately thread onto skewers with mushrooms. Proceed as directed in step 2.

ROASTED SHANGHAI PEPPER SALAD

1 jar (14 to 15 ounces) roasted red or
   red and yellow peppers
1½ tablespoons soy sauce
1 tablespoon rice vinegar
1 tablespoon Oriental sesame oil
2 teaspoons honey
1 clove garlic, minced
   Romaine lettuce or spinach leaves
2 tablespoons coarsely chopped cilantro

1. Drain and rinse peppers; pat dry with paper towels. Cut peppers lengthwise into ½-inch strips; place in small bowl.

2. Combine soy sauce, vinegar, sesame oil, honey and garlic; mix well. Pour over peppers; cover and refrigerate at least 2 hours. Serve over lettuce leaves. Sprinkle with cilantro.

Makes 4 servings

Note: The salad will keep up to 1 week covered and refrigerated.

MOO SHU VEGETABLES

½ package dried black Chinese
    mushrooms (6 to 7 mushrooms)
2 tablespoons peanut or vegetable oil
2 cloves garlic, minced
2 cups shredded napa cabbage or green
    cabbage *or* preshredded cabbage or
    coleslaw mix
1 red bell pepper, cut into short, thin
    strips
1 cup fresh or rinsed, drained canned
    bean sprouts
2 large green onions, cut into short, thin
    strips
¼ cup hoisin sauce
⅓ cup plum sauce
8 flour tortillas (6 to 7 inches), warmed

1. Place mushrooms in small bowl; cover with warm water. Soak 20 minutes to soften. Drain; squeeze out excess water. Discard stems; slice caps.

2. Heat wok or large skillet over medium-high heat. Add oil; heat until hot. Add garlic; stir-fry 30 seconds.

3. Add cabbage, mushrooms and red pepper; stir-fry 3 minutes. Add bean sprouts and onions; stir-fry 2 minutes. Add hoisin sauce; stir-fry 30 seconds or until mixture is hot.

4. Spread about 2 teaspoons plum sauce on each tortilla. Spoon heaping ¼ cup vegetable mixture over sauce. Fold bottom of tortilla up over filling, then fold sides over filling.

Makes 8 servings

Note: For information on storing unused bean sprouts, see page 6.

STIR–FRIED SPINACH WITH GARLIC

2 teaspoons peanut or vegetable oil
1 large clove garlic, minced
6 cups packed fresh spinach leaves (about
    8 ounces)
2 teaspoons soy sauce
1 teaspoon rice vinegar
¼ teaspoon sugar
1 teaspoon toasted sesame seeds*

1. Heat wok or large skillet over medium-high heat. Add oil; heat until hot. Add garlic; cook 1 minute.

2. Add spinach, soy sauce, vinegar and sugar; stir-fry 1 to 2 minutes until spinach is wilted. Sprinkle with sesame seeds.

Makes 2 servings

*To toast sesame seeds, spread seeds in small skillet. Shake skillet over medium heat 2 minutes or until seeds begin to pop and turn golden.

MARINATED CUCUMBERS

1 large cucumber (about 12 ounces)
2 tablespoons *each* rice vinegar,
    vegetable oil and soy sauce
1½ teaspoons sugar
1 clove garlic, minced
¼ teaspoon crushed red pepper flakes

1. Score cucumber lengthwise with tines of fork. Cut in half lengthwise; scrape out and discard seeds. Cut crosswise into ⅛-inch slices; place in medium bowl.

2. Combine remaining ingredients in cup; pour over cucumber. Toss to coat. Cover and refrigerate at least 4 hours or up to 2 days.

Makes 4 to 6 servings

Moo Shu Vegetables

Buddha's Delight

BUDDHA'S DELIGHT

1 package (1 ounce) dried black Chinese
   mushrooms
1 package (about 12 ounces) firm tofu,
   drained
1 tablespoon peanut or vegetable oil
2 cups diagonally cut 1-inch asparagus
   pieces *or* 1 package (10 ounces)
   frozen cut asparagus, thawed and
   drained
1 medium onion, cut into thin wedges
2 cloves garlic, minced
½ cup chicken broth
3 tablespoons hoisin sauce
¼ cup coarsely chopped cilantro or thinly
   sliced green onions

1. Place mushrooms in small bowl; cover with warm water. Soak 20 minutes to soften. Drain, squeezing out excess water over fine strainer into measuring cup; reserve. Discard mushroom stems; slice caps.

2. Press tofu lightly between paper towels; cut into ¾-inch squares or triangles.

3. Heat wok or large skillet over medium-high heat. Add oil; heat until hot. Add asparagus, onion wedges and garlic; stir-fry 4 minutes for fresh or 3 minutes for frozen asparagus.

4. Add mushrooms, ¼ cup reserved mushroom liquid,* broth and hoisin sauce. Reduce heat to medium-low. Simmer, uncovered, until asparagus is crisp-tender, 2 to 3 minutes for fresh or 1 minute for frozen asparagus.

5. Stir in tofu; heat through, stirring occasionally. Ladle into shallow bowls. Sprinkle with cilantro.

Makes 2 main-dish or 4 side-dish servings

*Remaining mushroom liquid may be covered and refrigerated up to 3 days or frozen up to 3 months. It may be used in soups and stews.

SZECHUAN EGGPLANT

1 pound Oriental eggplants or regular
   eggplant, peeled
2 tablespoons peanut or vegetable oil
2 cloves garlic, minced
¼ teaspoon crushed red pepper flakes *or*
   ½ teaspoon hot chili oil
3 green onions, cut into 1-inch pieces
¼ cup hoisin sauce
¼ cup chicken broth
   Toasted sesame seeds* (optional)

1. Cut eggplants into ½-inch slices; cut each slice into 2×½-inch strips.

2. Heat wok or large nonstick skillet over medium-high heat. Add peanut oil; heat until hot. Add eggplant, garlic and crushed red pepper; stir-fry 7 minutes or until eggplant is very tender and browned.

3. Reduce heat to medium. Add onions, hoisin sauce and broth; stir-fry 2 minutes. Sprinkle with sesame seeds.

Makes 4 to 6 servings

*To toast sesame seeds, spread seeds in small skillet. Shake skillet over medium heat 2 minutes or until seeds begin to pop and turn golden.

CASHEW GREEN BEANS

1 package (10 ounces) frozen julienne-cut
    green beans, thawed and drained
1 tablespoon peanut or vegetable oil
1 small onion, cut into thin wedges
2 cloves garlic, minced
2 tablespoons oyster sauce
1 tablespoon rice vinegar
1 tablespoon honey
¼ cup coarsely chopped cashews or
    peanuts

1. Pat green beans dry with paper towels.

2. Heat wok or large skillet over medium-high heat. Add oil; heat until hot. Add onion and garlic; stir-fry 3 minutes.

3. Add beans; stir-fry 2 minutes. Add oyster sauce, vinegar and honey; stir-fry 1 minute or until heated through. Remove from heat; stir in cashews. *Makes 4 servings*

BRAISED ORIENTAL CABBAGE

½ small head green cabbage (about
    ½ pound)
 1 small head bok choy (about ¾ pound)
½ cup beef or chicken broth
 2 tablespoons soy sauce
 2 tablespoons rice vinegar
 1 tablespoon brown sugar
¼ teaspoon crushed red pepper flakes
    (optional)
 1 tablespoon water
 1 tablespoon cornstarch

1. Cut cabbage into 1-inch pieces. Cut woody stems from bok choy leaves; slice stems into ½-inch pieces. Cut tops of leaves into ½-inch slices.

2. Combine cabbage and bok choy stems in 10-inch skillet. Add broth, soy sauce, vinegar, brown sugar and crushed red pepper.

3. Bring to a boil over high heat. Reduce heat to medium. Cover and simmer 5 minutes or until vegetables are crisp-tender.

4. Blend water into cornstarch in cup until smooth. Stir into skillet. Cook and stir 1 minute or until sauce boils and thickens.

5. Stir in reserved bok choy leaves; cook 1 minute more.
Makes 4 to 6 servings

ORIENTAL SALAD SUPREME

¼ cup peanut or vegetable oil
¼ cup rice vinegar
 2 tablespoons brown sugar
½ medium unpeeled cucumber, halved and
    sliced
 6 cups torn romaine or leaf lettuce
 1 cup chow mein noodles
¼ cup peanut halves (optional)

1. Combine oil, vinegar and brown sugar in small bowl; whisk until sugar dissolves.* Toss with cucumbers. Marinate, covered, in the refrigerator up to 4 hours.

2. Just before serving, toss dressing with remaining ingredients.
Makes 4 servings

*At this point, dressing may be tossed with remaining ingredients and served immediately.

Chinese Sweet and Sour Vegetables

CHINESE SWEET AND SOUR VEGETABLES

3 cups broccoli florets
2 medium carrots, diagonally sliced
1 large red bell pepper, cut into short, thin strips
¼ cup water
2 teaspoons cornstarch
1 teaspoon sugar
⅓ cup unsweetened pineapple juice
1 tablespoon soy sauce
1 tablespoon rice vinegar
½ teaspoon Oriental sesame oil
¼ cup diagonally sliced green onions or chopped cilantro (optional)

1. Combine broccoli, carrots, and red pepper in large skillet with tight-fitting lid. Add water; bring to a boil over high heat. Reduce heat to medium. Cover and steam 4 minutes or until vegetables are crisp-tender.

2. Meanwhile, combine cornstarch and sugar in small bowl. Blend in pineapple juice, soy sauce and vinegar until smooth.

3. Transfer vegetables to colander; drain. Stir pineapple mixture and add to skillet. Cook and stir 2 minutes or until sauce boils and thickens.

4. Return vegetables to skillet; toss with sauce. Stir in sesame oil. Garnish with onions. *Makes 4 servings*

RICE & NOODLES

RICE NOODLES WITH PEPPERS

3½ ounces dried Chinese rice sticks or rice
    noodles
⅓ cup chicken broth
3 tablespoons soy sauce
2 tablespoons tomato paste
1 tablespoon peanut or vegetable oil
1 medium green bell pepper, cut into
    long, thin strips
1 medium red bell pepper, cut into long,
    thin strips
1 medium onion, cut into thin wedges
2 cloves garlic, minced

1. Place rice sticks in bowl; cover with warm water. Soak 15 minutes to soften. Drain; cut into 3-inch pieces.

2. Combine broth, soy sauce and tomato paste in cup.

3. Heat wok or large skillet over medium-high heat. Add oil; heat until hot. Add peppers, onion and garlic; stir-fry 4 to 5 minutes until vegetables are crisp-tender.

4. Stir in broth mixture; heat through. Add noodles; stir-fry 3 minutes or until heated through. *Makes 6 servings*

VEGETABLE FRIED RICE

1 tablespoon peanut or vegetable oil
1½ cups small broccoli florets
¾ cup chopped red bell pepper
3 cups chilled cooked white rice
2 tablespoons soy sauce
½ cup shredded carrot
½ teaspoon Oriental sesame oil (optional)
    Purple kale leaves (optional)

1. Heat large nonstick skillet over medium heat. Add peanut oil; heat until hot. Add broccoli and red pepper; stir-fry 3 minutes or until vegetables are crisp-tender.

2. Add rice and soy sauce; stir-fry 2 minutes. Add carrot; heat through. Stir in sesame oil. Serve rice mixture on kale-lined plates. *Makes 4 servings*

Top to Bottom: Rice Noodles with Peppers, Vegetable Fried Rice

Rice & Noodles ● LIGHT & EASY CHINESE **223**

SESAME NOODLE CAKE

4 ounces vermicelli or Chinese egg
  noodles
1 tablespoon soy sauce
1 tablespoon peanut or vegetable oil
½ teaspoon Oriental sesame oil

1. Cook vermicelli according to package directions; drain well. Place in large bowl. Toss with soy sauce until sauce is absorbed.

2. Heat 10- or 11-inch nonstick skillet over medium heat. Add peanut oil; heat until hot. Add vermicelli mixture; pat into an even layer with spatula.

3. Cook, uncovered, 6 minutes or until bottom is lightly browned. Invert onto plate, then slide back into skillet, browned side up. Cook 4 minutes or until bottom is well-browned. Drizzle with sesame oil. Transfer to serving platter and cut into quarters.

Makes 4 servings

EGG FOO YUNG

2 eggs
2 egg whites
½ cup fresh or drained, rinsed canned
  bean sprouts
½ cup chopped fresh mushrooms
2 tablespoons thinly sliced green onion
2 tablespoons soy sauce, divided
1 tablespoon peanut or vegetable oil
1 cup chicken broth
1 tablespoon cornstarch
¼ teaspoon sugar
¼ teaspoon black pepper

1. Beat eggs with egg whites in large bowl. Stir in bean sprouts, mushrooms, onion and 1 tablespoon soy sauce.

2. Heat large nonstick skillet over medium-high heat. Add oil; heat until hot. To form each pancake, pour ¼ cup egg mixture into skillet (egg mixture will run; do not crowd skillet). Cook 1 to 2 minutes until bottoms of pancakes are set. Turn pancakes over; cook 1 to 2 minutes until pancakes are cooked through. Remove and keep warm. Repeat with remaining egg mixture.

3. Blend broth into cornstarch in small bowl until smooth. Stir into skillet. Stir in sugar and pepper; cook and stir 1 minute or until sauce boils and thickens.

4. Pour sauce over warm pancakes; serve immediately.

Makes 2 main-dish or 4 side-dish servings

Variation: Add ½ cup chopped cooked shrimp or ½ cup diced roasted pork to egg mixture.

Note: For information on storing unused bean sprouts, see page 6.

BEAN THREADS WITH TOFU AND VEGETABLES

8 ounces firm tofu, drained
4 tablespoons soy sauce, divided
1 tablespoon Oriental sesame oil
1 can (about 14 ounces) chicken broth
2 tablespoons dry sherry
1 package (3¾ ounces) bean threads
2 cups frozen mixed vegetable medley,
    such as broccoli, carrot and red
    pepper, thawed

1. Press tofu lightly between paper towels; cut into ¾-inch cubes or triangles. Place on shallow plate; drizzle with 1 tablespoon soy sauce and sesame oil.

2. Combine broth, remaining 3 tablespoons soy sauce and sherry in deep skillet or large saucepan. Bring to a boil; reduce heat. Add bean threads; simmer, uncovered, 7 minutes or until noodles absorb liquid, stirring occasionally to separate noodles.

3. Stir in vegetables; heat through. Stir in tofu mixture; cover and heat through, about 1 minute. *Makes 6 servings*

Note: For information on storing unused tofu, see page 7.

GINGER NOODLES WITH SESAME EGG STRIPS

2 egg whites
1 egg
3 tablespoons soy sauce, divided
3 teaspoons toasted sesame seeds,*
    divided
1 tablespoon peanut or vegetable oil
½ cup chicken broth
1 teaspoon minced fresh ginger
1 teaspoon Oriental sesame oil
6 ounces Chinese egg noodles or
    vermicelli, cooked and well drained
⅓ cup sliced green onions

1. Beat together egg whites, egg, 1 tablespoon soy sauce and 1 teaspoon sesame seeds in small bowl.

2. Heat large nonstick skillet over medium-high heat. Add peanut oil; heat until hot. Pour egg mixture into skillet; cook 1½ to 2 minutes or until bottom of omelet is set. Turn omelet over; cook 30 seconds to 1 minute. Slide out onto plate; cool and cut into ½-inch strips.

3. Add broth, remaining 2 tablespoons soy sauce, ginger and sesame oil to skillet. Bring to a boil; reduce heat. Add noodles; heat through. Add omelet strips and onions; heat through. Sprinkle with remaining 2 teaspoons sesame seeds.
Makes 4 servings

*To toast sesame seeds, spread seeds in small skillet. Shake skillet over medium heat 2 minutes or until seeds begin to pop and turn golden.

SINGAPORE RICE SALAD

1 can (8 ounces) pineapple tidbits or
    chunks in juice, undrained
3 cups chilled cooked white rice
1 cup diced cucumber
1 red bell pepper, diced
½ cup sliced green onions
½ cup shredded carrots
¼ cup peanut or vegetable oil
¼ cup teriyaki sauce
1 tablespoon fresh lime juice
    Chopped fresh cilantro (optional)
    Chopped peanuts or cashews (optional)
    Cucumber slices for garnish

1. Drain pineapple; reserve 3 tablespoons juice. Combine rice, diced cucumber, red pepper, onions, carrots and pineapple in large bowl.

2. Combine oil, teriyaki sauce, lime juice and reserved pineapple juice in small bowl; mix well. Pour over salad; toss to coat. Cover and refrigerate at least 2 hours or up to 12 hours. Sprinkle with cilantro and peanuts before serving. Garnish with cucumber slices. *Makes 6 to 8 servings*

ROASTED VEGETABLES WITH NOODLES

5 tablespoons soy sauce, divided
3 tablespoons peanut or vegetable oil
2 tablespoons rice vinegar
2 cloves garlic, minced
½ pound large fresh mushrooms
4 ounces shallots
1 medium zucchini squash, cut into 1-inch
    pieces, each cut into halves
1 medium yellow crookneck squash, cut
    into 1-inch pieces, each cut into
    halves
1 red bell pepper, cut into 1-inch pieces
1 yellow bell pepper, cut into 1-inch
    pieces
2 small Oriental eggplants, cut into
    ½-inch slices *or* 2 cups cubed
    eggplant
8 ounces Chinese egg noodles or
    vermicelli, hot cooked, drained
1 tablespoon Oriental sesame oil
1 teaspoon sugar

1. Preheat oven to 425°F. Combine 2 tablespoons soy sauce, peanut oil, vinegar and garlic in small bowl; mix well.

2. Combine vegetables in shallow roasting pan (do not line pan with foil). Toss with soy sauce mixture to coat well.

3. Roast vegetables 20 minutes or until browned and tender, stirring well after 10 minutes.

4. Place noodles in large bowl. Toss hot noodles with remaining 3 tablespoons soy sauce and sesame oil.

5. Toss roasted vegetables with noodle mixture; serve warm or at room temperature. *Makes 6 servings*

Singapore Rice Salad

ORIENTAL PILAF

1 medium onion, chopped
2 cloves garlic, minced
1 tablespoon peanut or vegetable oil
1 cup long-grain white rice
1 can (about 14 ounces) chicken or beef
    broth
¼ cup water*
3 ounces (1 cup) fresh snow peas, cut
    lengthwise into thin strips
2 medium carrots, coarsely shredded

1. Cook and stir onion and garlic in oil in medium saucepan over medium heat 4 minutes or until tender. Add rice; cook and stir 1 minute.

2. Add broth and water. Bring to a boil over high heat. Reduce heat to low. Cover and simmer 18 minutes. Stir in snow peas and carrots. Cover and simmer 2 minutes or until liquid is absorbed.

3. Let stand, covered, 5 minutes; fluff with fork before serving.

Makes 4 to 6 servings

*If using converted rice, increase water to ½ cup.

SZECHUAN COLD NOODLES

8 ounces vermicelli, broken in half or
    Chinese egg noodles
3 tablespoons soy sauce
2 tablespoons peanut or vegetable oil
3 tablespoons rice vinegar
1 large clove garlic, minced
1 teaspoon minced fresh ginger
1 teaspoon Oriental sesame oil (optional)
½ teaspoon crushed Szechuan peppercorns
    or crushed red pepper flakes
½ cup coarsely chopped cilantro (optional)
¼ cup chopped peanuts

1. Cook vermicelli according to package directions; drain.

2. Combine soy sauce, peanut oil, vinegar, garlic, ginger, sesame oil and peppercorns in large bowl. Add hot vermicelli; toss to coat. Sprinkle with cilantro and peanuts. Serve at room temperature or chilled.

Makes 4 servings

Variation: For *Szechuan Vegetable Noodles,* add 1 cup chopped peeled cucumber, ½ cup *each* chopped red bell pepper and sliced green onions and an additional 1 tablespoon soy sauce.

CANTONESE RICE CAKE PATTIES

2 cups chilled cooked white rice
⅓ cup chopped red bell pepper
¼ cup thinly sliced green onions
2 tablespoons soy sauce
2 egg whites, slightly beaten
1 egg, slightly beaten
3 tablespoons peanut or vegetable oil,
    divided

1. Mix rice, red pepper, onions, soy sauce, egg whites and egg in medium bowl.

2. Heat large nonstick skillet over medium heat. Add 1 tablespoon oil; heat until hot. For each patty, spoon ⅓ cup rice mixture into skillet; flatten patties slightly with back of spatula. Cook patties, 3 at a time, 3 to 4 minutes until bottoms are golden brown. Turn patties over; cook 3 minutes or until golden brown. Keep patties warm in 200°F oven. Repeat with remaining oil and rice mixture.

Makes about 6 servings (about 9 patties)

CURRIED NOODLES

7 ounces dried Chinese rice sticks or rice
    noodles
1 tablespoon peanut or vegetable oil
1 large red bell pepper, cut into short,
    thin strips
2 large green onions, cut into ½-inch
    pieces
1 clove garlic, minced
1 teaspoon minced fresh ginger
2 teaspoons curry powder
⅛ to ¼ teaspoon crushed red pepper
    flakes
½ cup chicken broth
2 tablespoons soy sauce

1. Place rice sticks in bowl; cover with warm water. Soak 15 minutes to soften. Drain; cut into 3-inch pieces.

2. Heat wok or large skillet over medium-high heat. Add oil; heat until hot. Add red pepper strips; stir-fry 3 minutes.

3. Add onions, garlic and ginger; stir-fry 1 minute. Add curry powder and crushed red pepper; stir-fry 1 minute.

4. Add broth and soy sauce; heat through. Add noodles; stir-fry 3 minutes or until heated through. *Makes 6 servings*

VEGETABLE LO MEIN

8 ounces vermicelli, thin spaghetti or
    Chinese mein noodles, cooked and
    drained
1½ tablespoons Oriental sesame oil
2 teaspoons peanut or vegetable oil
2 teaspoons minced fresh ginger
2 cups sliced bok choy
1 cup fresh or drained, rinsed canned
    bean sprouts
½ cup chicken broth
2 tablespoons oyster sauce
1 tablespoon soy sauce

1. Toss vermicelli with sesame oil in large bowl to coat well.

2. Heat large nonstick skillet over medium heat. Add peanut oil; heat until hot. Stir in ginger.

3. Add bok choy; stir-fry 3 to 4 minutes or until crisp-tender. Add bean sprouts; stir-fry 1 minute.

4. Stir in broth, oyster sauce and soy sauce; mix well. Add vermicelli mixture; heat through, stirring until liquid is absorbed.
Makes 6 servings

Note: For information on storing unused bean sprouts, see page 6.

Cellophane Noodle Salad

CELLOPHANE NOODLE SALAD

1 package (3¾ ounces) bean threads
2 tablespoons peanut or vegetable oil
8 ounces medium or large raw shrimp,
    peeled, deveined
3 cloves garlic, minced
¼ teaspoon crushed red pepper flakes
½ cup cooked pork or ham strips
    (optional)
2 tablespoons soy sauce
1 tablespoon fresh lemon juice
1 tablespoon rice vinegar
1 tablespoon Oriental sesame oil
⅓ cup thinly sliced green onions or
    coarsely chopped cilantro

1. Place bean threads in medium bowl; cover with warm water. Soak 15 minutes to soften. Drain well; cut into 2-inch pieces.

2. Heat wok or large skillet over medium-high heat. Add peanut oil; heat until hot. Add shrimp, garlic and crushed red pepper; stir-fry 2 minutes. Add pork, soy sauce, lemon juice, vinegar and sesame oil; stir-fry 1 minutes.

3. Add bean threads; stir-fry 1 minute or until heated through. Serve warm, chilled or at room temperature. Sprinkle with onions before serving.
Makes 4 servings

PORK FRIED RICE

1 egg
1 egg white
1 tablespoon *plus* 2 teaspoons peanut or
    vegetable oil, divided
3 cups chilled cooked white rice
2 tablespoons stir-fry sauce
1 cup diced cooked pork*
½ cup frozen baby peas or drained canned
    peas
½ cup thinly sliced green onions

1. Beat egg with egg white in small bowl.

2. Heat large nonstick skillet over medium-high heat. Add 2 teaspoons oil; heat until hot. Add eggs, tilting skillet to coat surface. Cook 2 minutes or until eggs are set and lightly browned on bottom. Transfer to plate.

3. Heat remaining 1 tablespoon oil in skillet. Add rice and stir-fry sauce; mix well. Stir in pork, peas and onions; heat through, stirring frequently.

4. Cut egg pancake into short, thin strips. Gently stir into rice mixture; heat through.
Makes 2 main-dish or 4 side-dish servings

*Or, substitute 1 cup small cooked shrimp, diced cooked beef or chicken for the pork.

INDEX

R

Rice
Cantonese Rice Cake Patties, 228
Celebration Pork & Rice, 32
Fried Rice, 148
New Year Fried Rice, 78
Oriental Pilaf, 228
Pagoda Fried Rice, 81
Pork Fried Rice, 231
Shrimp Fried Rice, 74
Singapore Rice Salad, 226
Steamed Rice, 151
Vegetable Fried Rice, 222
Vegetarian Fried Rice, 155
Rice Noodles with Peppers, 222
Roasted Pork, 173
Roasted Shanghai Pepper Salad, 215
Roasted Vegetables with Noodles, 226

S

Salad Dressings
Lemon-Soy Dressing, 81
Soy-Sesame Dressing, 153
Salads
Bean Sprout & Spinach Salad, 79
Cantonese Chicken Salad, 74
Cellophane Noodle Salad, 231
Chinese Chicken Salad, 123, 196
"Crab" & Cucumber Noodle Salad, 80
Firecracker Salad, 76
Hot Oriental Salad, 77
Mandarin Chicken Salad, 59
Orange-Onion Salad, 215
Oriental Chicken & Cabbage Salad, 81
Oriental Salad Supreme, 220
Roasted Shanghai Pepper Salad, 215
Sesame Chicken Salad, 120
Singapore Rice Salad, 226
Soy-Spinach Salad, 81
Sprout-Cucumber Salad, 78
Szechuan Chicken Salad with Peanut Dressing, 194
Szechuan Pork Salad, 78
Satay Beef, 103
Sauces
Braised Lion's Head Sauce, 105
Crab Sauce, 132

Sauces *(continued)*
Curry Sauce, 129
Dipping Sauce, 179
Lemon Sauce, 119
Mandarin Peach Sauce, 37
Orange-Plum Sauce, 54
Plum Sauce, 29
Sesame Sauce, 109
Sweet and Sour Sauce, 88
Tempura Dipping Sauce, 63
Saucy Shrimp, 22
Saucy Shrimp over Chinese Noodle Cakes, 71
Scallops with Vegetables, 139
Seafood and Vegetable Tempura, 63
Seafood Combination, 135
Sesame Cheese Crackers, 13
Sesame Chicken, 200
Sesame Chicken Salad, 120
Sesame Noodle Cake, 224
Sesame Sauce, 109
Sesame-Garlic Flank Steak, 173
Shanghai Chicken with Asparagus and Ham, 199
Shanghai Shrimp Stir-Fry, 64
Shanghai Steamed Fish, 209
Shanghai Sweet & Sour Fish, 73
Shantung Chicken, 57
Shantung Twin Mushroom Soup, 161
Shellfish *(see also* **Shrimp***)*
Clams in Black Bean Sauce, 137
"Crab" & Cucumber Noodle Salad, 80
Crab Cakes Canton, 162
Crab Combination Soup, 91
Crab in Ginger Sauce, 131
Crab-Stuffed Shrimp, 128
Easy Seafood Stir-Fry, 209
Fish Rolls with Crab Sauce, 132
Fragrant Braised Oysters, 130
Mongolian Hot Pot, 179
Orange-Almond Scallops, 205
Scallops with Vegetables, 139
Seafood and Vegetable Tempura, 63
Seafood Combination, 135
Stir-Fried Crab, 202
Szechuan Squid Stir-Fry, 73
Shrimp
Braised Shrimp with Vegetables, 132
Butterfly Shrimp, 135
Cellophane Noodle Salad, 231
Chicken Chow Mein, 120
Chilled Shrimp in Chinese Mustard Sauce, 158

Shrimp *(continued)*
Chinese Porcupine Meatballs, 62
Crab-Stuffed Shrimp, 128
Crystal Shrimp with Sweet & Sour Sauce, 60
Drunken Shrimp, 66
Easy Seafood Stir-Fry, 209
Five-Spice Shrimp with Walnuts, 210
Fried Rice, 148
Garlic Skewered Shrimp, 205
Hors d'Oeuvre Rolls, 91
Hot and Sour Shrimp, 206
Lo Mein Noodles with Shrimp, 150
Mongolian Hot Pot, 179
Prawns-in-Shell, 13
Saucy Shrimp, 22
Saucy Shrimp over Chinese Noodle Cakes, 71
Seafood and Vegetable Tempura, 63
Seafood Combination, 135
Shanghai Shrimp Stir-Fry, 64
Shrimp & Vegetable Stir-Fry, 68
Shrimp Fried Rice, 74
Shrimp Omelets, 139
Shrimp Teriyaki, 14
Shrimp Toast, 84, 161
Shrimp-in-Shell, 67
Shrimp-Stuffed Bean Curd, 143
Shrimp & Vegetable Stir-Fry, 68
Shrimp Fried Rice, 74
Shrimp Omelets, 139
Shrimp Teriyaki, 14
Shrimp Toast, 84, 161
Shrimp-in-Shell, 67
Shrimp-Stuffed Bean Curd, 143
Side Dishes
Bean Curd with Oyster Sauce, 146
Bean Threads with Minced Pork, 154
Bean Threads with Tofu and Vegetables, 225
Braised Choice Vegetables, 147
Braised Oriental Cabbage, 220
Buddha's Delight, 219
Cantonese Rice Cake Patties, 228
Cashew Green Beans, 220
Chinese Mixed Pickled Vegetables, 140
Chinese Noodle Cakes, 71
Chinese Sweet and Sour Vegetables, 221
Chinese Vegetables, 145
Cold Stirred Noodles, 153

METRIC CONVERSION CHART

VOLUME MEASUREMENTS (dry)

¹/₈ teaspoon = 0.5 mL
¹/₄ teaspoon = 1 mL
¹/₂ teaspoon = 2 mL
³/₄ teaspoon = 4 mL
1 teaspoon = 5 mL
1 tablespoon = 15 mL
2 tablespoons = 30 mL
¹/₄ cup = 60 mL
¹/₃ cup = 75 mL
¹/₂ cup = 125 mL
²/₃ cup = 150 mL
³/₄ cup = 175 mL
1 cup = 250 mL
2 cups = 1 pint = 500 mL
3 cups = 750 mL
4 cups = 1 quart = 1 L

VOLUME MEASUREMENTS (fluid)

1 fluid ounce (2 tablespoons) = 30 mL
4 fluid ounces (¹/₂ cup) = 125 mL
8 fluid ounces (1 cup) = 250 mL
12 fluid ounces (1¹/₂ cups) = 375 mL
16 fluid ounces (2 cups) = 500 mL

WEIGHTS (mass)

¹/₂ ounce = 15 g
1 ounce = 30 g
3 ounces = 90 g
4 ounces = 120 g
8 ounces = 225 g
10 ounces = 285 g
12 ounces = 360 g
16 ounces = 1 pound = 450 g

DIMENSIONS

¹/₁₆ inch = 2 mm
¹/₈ inch = 3 mm
¹/₄ inch = 6 mm
¹/₂ inch = 1.5 cm
³/₄ inch = 2 cm
1 inch = 2.5 cm

OVEN TEMPERATURES

250°F = 120°C
275°F = 140°C
300°F = 150°C
325°F = 160°C
350°F = 180°C
375°F = 190°C
400°F = 200°C
425°F = 220°C
450°F = 230°C

BAKING PAN SIZES

Utensil	Size in Inches/Quarts	Metric Volume	Size in Centimeters
Baking or	8 × 8 × 2	2 L	20 × 20 × 5
Cake Pan	9 × 9 × 2	2.5 L	22 × 22 × 5
(square or	12 × 8 × 2	3 L	30 × 20 × 5
rectangular)	13 × 9 × 2	3.5 L	33 × 23 × 5
Loaf Pan	8 × 4 × 3	1.5 L	20 × 10 × 7
	9 × 5 × 3	2 L	23 × 13 × 7
Round Layer	8 × 1½	1.2 L	20 × 4
Cake Pan	9 × 1½	1.5 L	23 × 4
Pie Plate	8 × 1¼	750 mL	20 × 3
	9 × 1¼	1 L	23 × 3
Baking Dish	1 quart	1 L	—
or Casserole	1½ quart	1.5 L	—
	2 quart	2 L	—